THE *Essential*

SOUTHWEST COOKBOOK

Edited by MARILYN NOBLE, SUSAN LOWELL, *and* CAROLINE COOK

RIO NUEVO
PUBLISHERS
Tucson, Arizona

RIO NUEVO PUBLISHERS®
P.O. Box 5250
Tucson, Arizona 85703-0250
520-623-9558
www.rionuevo.com

Cover design: DAVID JENNEY
Design: KATIE JENNINGS

Cover photos: © Rita Maas/Foodpix/Getty Images
All photos by Robin Stancliff except pp. iv, 3, 6, 11, 30, 44, 46, 50, 60, 65, 76, 103, 139, 154, 163: W. Ross Humphreys; p. i: Shutterstock/Africa Studio; p. 6: Shutterstock/Larina Natalia; p. 72: Shutterstock/svry

Printed in China

10   9   8   7   6

Library of Congress Cataloging-in-Publication Data

Noble, Marilyn.
  The essential Southwest cookbook / [Marilyn Noble, Susan Lowell, Caroline Cook]
     pages cm
  Includes index.
  ISBN-13: 978-1-933855-90-5
  ISBN-10: 1-933855-90-8
1. Cooking, American--Southwestern style. I. Lowell, Susan, 1950- II. Cook, Caroline. III. Title.
  TX715.2.S69N625 2013
  641.5979—dc23
     2013029288

The recipes contained in this book are to be followed exactly as written. Neither the publisher nor the author is responsible for your specific health or allergy needs that may require medical supervision, or for any adverse reactions to the recipes contained in this book.

CONTENTS

7 » TORTILLAS • *Breads and Spoons*

These simple flatbreads play many roles in Southwest cuisine, from staff of life to eating utensil. But whether hot from the griddle or richly embellished, corn and wheat tortillas are absolutely fundamental. Here's a wide range of classic tortilla-based recipes: tacos, tostadas, burritos, enchiladas, nachos, and many more.

31 » CHILES • *The Essential Spark*

Green or ripe, fresh or dried, subtly flavored or stunningly hot, chile peppers join with other native American crops, such as corn, beans, squash, and tomatoes, to give Southwestern food its distinctive taste and glow. Here you will find recipes for chiles stuffed, grilled, stewed, sprinkled, or appetizingly diffused throughout a dish.

45 » SALSAS & SAUCES • *Savor and Flavor*

Whether freshly chopped (like pico de gallo) or mashed (like guacamole) or pureed (like salsa verde) or long-simmered (like New Mexico red and green), lively, colorful sauces are as indispensable as tortillas and chiles to the Southwest kitchen.

61 » BEANS & RICE • *Southwestern Staples*

These foods are filling, nutritious, long-lasting in the pantry, and modest in price. But it's their satisfying taste and versatility that make them most welcome, in dishes ranging from wonderful vegetarian main courses to colorful rice on the side.

73 » MEATS, POULTRY & FISH • *The Grill and the Stove*

The Southwest has a long barbecue tradition, which is well represented here in recipes for fish, poultry, and various meats. We also include characteristic stews, braises, sausages, eggs, and entrée salads.

101 » CORN & SQUASH • *The Ancient Crops*

We can't live by corn alone, good as it is. Meat and vegetables such as squash and beans improve it nutritionally. But together, they work some magic to make such combinations even more delicious in soups, entrees, vegetable dishes, and pancakes.

123 » CITRUS & OTHER FRUIT • *Sweet and Sour Power*

An array of fruit flavors weave their way through Southwestern cuisine, beginning with cool drinks, moving to main courses (in ceviche, for example, citrus juice "cooks" fish), and finishing up with piquant fruit desserts.

137 » DESSERTS • *Light and Dark Delights*

Chocolate is native to Central America, and it features frequently in these recipes—sometimes enhanced by two other American flavors, vanilla and chile. Simple custards, cakes, fruit desserts, and fruit ices are also favorite ways to end a spicy meal.

157 » DRINKS • *Liquid Fiestas*

As a finale, here's a selection of refreshing, lightly spirited beverages infused with Southwestern style, including the perfect margarita, your very own coffee liqueur, and white as well as red sangria.

INTRODUCTION

Taste the Southwest.

If you cook these recipes you will discover its essence. Even if you're far away, lost, and blindfolded, you can't mistake it. First, the aromas are irresistible: lush, herbal, spicy, toasted. And then come the flavors—a mix of milky corn, meaty beans, soft sweet squash, piquant onions and tomatoes—all seasoned with a whiff of smoke, touched with buttery melted cheese, and sparked with the nip and the lingering glow of chile. That's the essence of the Southwest.

Somehow, this marvelous food is exotic and homey at the same time. In fact, the ingredients for Southwestern cooking are easy to find, and the basic recipes are simple to prepare. Many could be cooked in minutes on a campfire. It's the taste that's special.

And no wonder, for Southwestern cuisine is the longest continuous culinary tradition in the United States. For thousands of years these regional foods have been grown and cooked in the same places, with very much the same techniques. New foods arrived as the centuries went by, of course. And recipes have been perfected.

Rich in flavors, Southwestern food enjoys an equally rich cultural heritage, starting more than 10,000 years ago and still simmering along in the same geography. Ancient Southwesterners hunted game and gathered wild greens, herbs, nuts, seeds, chiles, and cactus fruit. All of these foods are still ingredients in the traditional cooking of Arizona, New Mexico, southern Utah and Colorado, parts of Texas and California, and northern Mexico.

Corn, beans, squash, peppers, and domesticated turkeys arrived somewhat later from what are now Mexico and Central America. By the year 1000, the Southwestern menu probably included roasted and dried meats, spicy stews and soups, salsas, and the forerunners of tortillas, tamales, enchiladas, tacos, tostadas, and posole, as well as corn mush, dumplings, popcorn, puddings, sweets, and beverages, including some produced from cacti and agaves.

Spaniards entered the Southwest in the 1530s, bringing important additions to the local diet, such as wheat, melons, fruits, beef, pork, and mutton. Besides ranching and new kinds of farming, they introduced bread ovens and metal knives, grills, and cookware. Under Spanish and Mexican influence, more Mesoamerican crops such as tomatoes and avocados also appeared. Then in the nineteenth century Anglo-Americans and industrialization transformed the region, a process that continues today. But a modern emphasis on local, healthful, and heirloom foods now reconnects Southwestern cooks with their heritage in many good ways.

Lately, some Southwestern specialties have traveled far from their origins, but as commercial and fast food they have not traveled well. To achieve true glory, we urge you to take fresh ingredients and make your own salsas, corn chips, tacos, and beans. Whip up real hot chocolate. Make a perfectly limey margarita. The effort is minimal, but the genuine flavors will amaze you.

In these pages you will find Southwestern classics both ancient and modern (for this historic cuisine continues to develop in exciting new ways). We have selected more than a hundred of the best recipes we know, mostly from regional cookbooks published by Rio Nuevo Publishers over the last two decades, and we have organized them by fundamental ingredients. Each chapter revolves around one of these essentials of Southwestern cuisine and presents basic information as well as a set of indispensable dishes.

From appetizers to after-dinner drinks, from tortilla soup to piñon nuts, we promise that *The Essential Southwest Cookbook* will guide, delight, and feed you very, very well.

Marilyn Noble, Susan Lowell, Caroline Cook

A NOTE ON CHILES

Many of these recipes include suggested amounts of chile. But chiles vary, and not everyone likes chiles equally hot! Chile seeds and inner pith contain most of the chemical capsaicin, which causes the characteristic burn, so you can remove and discard them to tame the final result. If you are at all in doubt, start with half the suggested amount, then taste, and gradually increase the chile. You can also taste a very tiny amount of chile before you add it, or sometimes a quick whiff will give you a sense of its potency. This is much easier than trying to cool down a dish that's already on fire. And die-hards can always add more chile at the table if they wish.

Best remedies for a chile overdose: a mouthful of a dairy product, lettuce, or bland food. Water won't do much, nor will ice. In fact, the use of "hot" or "heat" (as in temperature) to describe the effect of chile is common but inaccurate. The real sensation of capsaicin is more like a jellyfish or chemical sting, or a mild but persistent electric shock. For more information on handling chiles, see the Chile section on page 31.

COMMON VARIETIES

Anaheim • Also known as the California green chile, this long shiny green chile is among the mildest and sweetest of the commonly used varieties.

Ancho • A dried poblano, the ancho has a smoky sweet flavor. It is among the most widely used chiles in Mexico.

Chile de árbol • A skinny, thin-fleshed, red chile, the dried árbol brings a sharp, hot-pepper essence to any dish it touches. It is commonly used to put the burn in hot sauce.

Chiltepín • A wild, round, extremely hot red or green pepper about the size of a small pea, this is the only chile native to the United States. A domesticated variety is called chile pequín.

Chipotle • A dried, smoked jalapeño, the chipotle has intense heat. Its smoky flavor infuses any food with which it is prepared.

Habanero • A truly beautiful chile, the habanero ripens from green to yellow to brilliant orange. Habaneros are intensely hot.

Jalapeño • Picked green and served fresh or pickled, the jalapeño is probably the most widely available chile in the United States. Somewhat mild on the heat scale when green, as it ripens to red, the heat intensifies. Ripened and smoked, it becomes the chipotle.

New Mexico (also known as **Hatch** or **Chimayo**, depending on where they're grown) • A large chile, it resembles the Anaheim but can be hotter. They can be used green or ripened to red, dried, and hung in strands or *ristras.*

Pasilla (Negro) • The dried pasilla, often called *chile negro,* offers a sharp bite. A large pepper, almost black in color, it can be used fresh for almost anything from stuffing to frying whole.

Poblano • A large, triangular chile, the poblano is a sweet, thin-skinned variety with pleasant heat. Fresh, it is commonly served stuffed; dried, it becomes the ancho.

Serrano • A small, fresh chile with smooth skin, the serrano's heat level ranges from hot to absolute fire.

A WORD ABOUT CHILE POWDER: Be sure to look for pure chile powder. Sometimes when you buy it in the grocery store, it has other ingredients such as salt, cumin, garlic powder, or oregano, all of which can drastically change the flavor profile of the recipe.

CHEESE AND CREAM

Asadero • A mild white Mexican cheese that melts well. Substitute cheddar, Monterey Jack, mozzarella, or a mixture.

Cheddar • Either a yellow or a white cheese that melts readily. Mild or longhorn style is a favorite across the Southwest, but sharp cheddar is uncharacteristic.

Cotija • A semi-hard, crumbly, salty, aged, somewhat sharp white cheese favored for toppings. It can be grated, and when more fully aged, it is called *añejo*. Substitute dry feta, Parmesan, or Romano.

Crema • A slightly sour, pourable cream similar to French crème fraîche. It's often available in supermarket dairy cases, but you can also substitute commercial sour cream thinned with milk or cream, or plain heavy cream, or crème fraîche.

Fresco • A snow-white, creamy, moist cheese like farmer's or pot cheese, which can be substituted for it. It has a short shelf life.

Monterey Jack • Readily available in American supermarkets, a cheese often chosen for its delicate flavor and good melting quality. Pepper Jack, flavored with jalapeños, also turns up in Southwestern recipes.

Mozzarella • Another good melting cheese that can stand in for asadero or cheddar, though it is less flavorful.

Oaxaca • A mild, stringy white cheese often sold in rope shapes. A close kin to mozzarella.

Panela • Its soft, curdy texture and milky flavor resemble cottage cheese or Indian paneer cheese.

Ranchero • A mild white cheese that crumbles well for toppings and softens with heat, but does not melt into strings.

SOUTHWESTERN FLAVORS

Achiote • The red seeds of this tropical American shrub produce both a spice and a yellow food colorant called *annatto*, sold either as a powder or a paste.

Anise • A Mediterranean herb with licorice-flavored seeds, which are used in the Southwest to flavor biscochitos and other confections, including hot chocolate.

Cilantro • In Southwestern cuisine, this Spanish word usually refers to the fresh green leaves of the coriander plant, native to southern Europe, North Africa, and southwestern Asia. Fresh cilantro has a strong herbal flavor that appeals to most palates but seems unpleasant to others. It is usually added raw just before serving, as its flavor fades when cooked, dried, or frozen. Tasting very differently of citrus and spice, coriander seeds are used in pastry, curries, and pickles.

Cinnamon and Canela • Different types of cinnamon come from the inner bark of several different species of trees native to Southeast Asia. The cheapest, most pungent, and also most common cinnamon on grocery shelves is actually cassia. Epicures consider canela or *Cinnamomum verum* (true cinnamon, a product of Sri Lanka) to have the most delicate flavor, and it is preferred in Mexico and the Southwest. Canela also has a much softer texture than cassia and is easy to grate or pulverize. Cassia sticks will break your blender.

Cumin • A warm, earthy-tasting spice produced from the seeds of Cuminum cyminum, a member of the parsley family. Cumin originated in the Middle East and India but now grows worldwide.

Epazote • A native American plant with distinctive jagged leaves and a distinctive herbal, medicinal taste. Because epazote is also reputed to reduce the gassy side effects of beans, it is often cooked with them, particularly black beans. It can be used fresh or dry.

Mexican Oregano • Closely related to common oregano and marjoram, which belong to the mint family, Mexican oregano is actually a vervein (like lemon verbena). It tastes lighter and less piney than Italian or Greek oregano, but ordinary oregano can substitute, perhaps in slightly smaller quantities.

Vanilla • A precious, perfumy flavoring created from the pods of orchids native to Mexico. The second most expensive spice in the world after saffron, vanilla is yet another great gift to world gastronomy from the American tropics, along with corn, squash, tomatoes, potatoes, chiles, and chocolate.

TORTILLAS

TORTILLAS ARE THE ORIGINAL BREAD OF THE AMERICAS, with a history that stretches all the way back to pre-Columbian times. The indigenous version was made from corn, but the Europeans brought wheat flour to the New World, and soon flour tortillas were a staple, too. Tortillas are versatile and can replace bread or crackers at almost any meal—they can be eaten cold or warm, baked or fried, wrapped around everything from beans to steak to fish or even salad, and enjoyed plain or with a little pat of butter and drizzle of honey.

You can find acceptable corn and flour tortillas in most grocery stores, but quality and freshness make a big difference in this simple, essential food. It's worth searching out a tortillería (tortilla bakery) or Latino supermarket, if you are lucky enough to live in a region where these exist. There you may find a range of sizes and perhaps also chubby gorditas, which are thicker and richer than plain tortillas. Occasionally, an entrepreneurial cook will sell homemade tortillas, which should be gratefully enjoyed whenever possible. Southwestern or Mexican restaurants sometimes sell tortillas as well, and if none of these is possible, look for a busy supermarket with good turnover.

But tortillas taste wonderful when you make them yourself. It takes some practice to roll the masa (dough) into the right shape and thickness. In fact, a traditional joke is that a beginner's tortillas resemble the shape of the cook's home state (Arizona, Texas, Sonora, etc.). But they taste just as good as the perfectly round ones, and once you do it a few times, you'll get the hang of it. And you might never buy tortillas at the grocery store again.

Corn Tortillas

2 cups masa harina

1½–2 cups warm water

½ teaspoon salt

QUAKER MASA HARINA IS ONE OF SEVERAL BRAND NAMES for finely ground flour that comes from limed corn, and "masa harina" is often used casually as a term for corn flour itself. Masa is any kind of dough, so literally the words mean "dough flour." These products are available at most grocery stores. You can also use moist, fresh corn masa if you can find it. With fresh masa, you just add some salt and skip the kneading step. Either one is fine.

» Pour the masa harina into a bowl and add warm water and salt. Stir to mix and then allow to sit for several minutes. Begin to knead the dough with your fingers until it comes together in a smooth mound. If it's too dry, add a little water. If it's sticky, add a little more masa harina. When the dough is ready, pinch off pieces about the size of a golf ball and roll into balls. Keep them covered so they don't dry out.

» Experienced cooks rapidly pat out tortillas between their palms, but most beginners find that pressing is easier. To press, use a tortilla press or a large heavy plate. Lay a sheet of waxed paper on the work surface and place the ball of dough in the middle. Top with another sheet of wax paper and then press down with the plate until the tortilla is flattened and about six inches in diameter.

» Heat a griddle (called a *comal* in Spanish) over medium high heat, remove the wax paper, and gently place the tortilla in the center. Allow to cook until lightly browned, about 30 seconds. Turn and brown the other side. Remove from the heat and wrap in a warm dish towel. Repeat until all of the tortillas are cooked.

» Store in a plastic zipper bag after they've cooled.

Makes about 18

Flour Tortillas

TORTILLAS ARE GREAT RIGHT OFF THE GRIDDLE, especially smeared with butter, so expect them to be stolen very quickly if left unguarded. Children love them. You'll find that you can double, triple, and even quadruple this recipe with no loss of quality, once you have learned to mix and handle the dough.

» Combine the dry ingredients in a large bowl, add the shortening, and blend very thoroughly with a pastry blender, two dinner knives, or your fingertips. Add water in small increments and knead the dough until it is smooth and pliable. If the dough is not well blended, the tortillas will be brittle instead of pliable, but if it is blended too much they may be a little tough.

» Form bolitas (little balls of tortilla dough) of equal size, about the size of walnuts. Then cover with a damp towel and let them sit for 10 or 15 minutes.

» Meanwhile, heat the griddle to medium high or until a drop of water sizzles away instantly.

» Rolling: This is the part that takes some practice. First, dust the rolling pin and the surface area (as close to the griddle as possible) with a light, even layer of flour. Put the bolita in the middle of the floured area and flatten it into as round a shape as possible by rolling and then turning the rolled disk over several times to keep it an even thickness and symmetrically round.

» After the tortilla is rolled, lift it carefully with your fingertips and set it on the dry medium-hot griddle. Watch closely until little bubbles form on the tops of each tortilla. By lifting the edge slightly, you'll be able to turn it over carefully and quickly with your fingertips to cook evenly on both sides. (Fingers are easiest for this and you won't risk tearing the tortilla with tongs or a fork.) Place the cooked tortillas on a towel beside your rolling area to let them cool slightly before stacking, otherwise they will stick together. Store them inside a towel in a closed container until served.

Makes 5-6 large or 12 small tortillas

4 cups unbleached flour

1½ teaspoons baking powder

1 teaspoon salt

3 tablespoons shortening or lard

1 to 1½ cups warm water

Tortilla Chips

½ cup oil or lard for frying

12 corn or flour tortillas, 6-inch, cut into 8 wedges each

Sea salt

FRESH, HOT TORTILLA CHIPS RIGHT OFF THE STOVE, sprinkled with a little sea salt and maybe even a little splash of lime juice, are one of the best snacks ever. Pair them with a good salsa or guacamole and you may not even need to eat dinner.

» Pour the oil into the bottom of a cast iron skillet to a depth of about ⅛ inch. Heat over medium high until the oil is shimmering. Place the tortilla wedges in batches into the oil in a single layer and fry until light brown and crisp, turning as necessary. Remove to a paper towel–lined plate. Sprinkle with a light layer of salt to taste. If you need to add a little more oil between batches, wait until it comes up to temperature before adding more tortillas.

» While each successive batch is cooking, place the previous batch into a basket or bowl, and cover the plate with new paper towels, if necessary.

VARIATION Baked Tortilla Chips

» Preheat the oven to 400 degrees F. Instead of pouring the oil into a skillet, use a pastry brush to coat both sides of each tortilla. Cut them into wedges and place them on a large baking pan or cookie sheet. Sprinkle with salt. Bake for 10–15 minutes, turning at least once. Remove from the oven and place in a bowl or basket for serving. These aren't fat-free, but they require less oil than the fried version.

Nachos

THIS RECIPE APPEARED IN THE SIXTIES OR SEVENTIES. Suddenly, people were serving cheese-covered chips and putting all kinds of good things on top. Nachos are easy to do on the spur of the moment or when you need a quick nutritious snack for children or company. Toppings can be as simple as a sprinkle of cheese or as lavish as the ones in this recipe.

» Preheat the oven to 350 degrees F.

» Spread the tortilla chips on a baking sheet and layer evenly with beans and chile. Heat in the oven for 10 minutes, top with grated cheese, return to the oven, and bake for 3 to 5 more minutes.

» Move the chips with a spatula to a serving dish and garnish with jalapeños and tomatoes. You can also drop a dollop of sour cream on top of it all and then decorate it with the chopped green onion.

Serves from 4 to 6 people

½ large bag of large tortilla chips

1 cup refried beans

½ cup finely chopped, roasted, peeled, and seeded green chile

½ pound longhorn cheese, grated

¼ cup thinly sliced jalapeños

½ cup diced tomatoes

Sour cream, optional

¼ cup finely chopped green onion, optional

Traditional Tacos

Oil for frying

12 corn tortillas

1 pound lean ground beef

½ teaspoon salt

½ teaspoon pepper

½ teaspoon chile powder

½ cup grated cheddar cheese

1 bunch green onions, white and
green parts sliced

2 tomatoes, chopped

1 small head lettuce, shredded

Salsa for garnish

IT'S SO EASY TO MAKE TACO SHELLS, you should never buy those prefab things that come in a cardboard box at the store. Use the freshest corn tortillas you can find and make sure the oil is hot enough. You'll have crunchy delicious taco shells in no time.

» Heat the oil in a small cast-iron skillet until shimmering. While the oil is heating, line a cookie sheet with paper towels. Once the oil is hot, dip a corn tortilla into it, using a fork to hold one side up to make a taco shell. When the side in the oil is crisp and brown, flip the tortilla and cook the other side. Use the fork to lift the shell from the pan and set on the cookie sheet open side down to drain. Repeat for remaining tortillas.

» After the shells are made, brown the ground beef in a skillet over medium heat. As the meat begins to brown, stir in the salt, pepper, and chile powder. When the meat is cooked, drain off any grease.

» Place a small amount of ground beef in each taco shell, followed by the cheese, green onions, tomatoes, and lettuce. Garnish with the salsa of your choice.

Makes 1 dozen

Roasted Pork Soft Tacos

TO MAKE SOFT TACOS, simply fold warm corn tortillas around the filling of your choice, such as this delectable combination. This recipe is a good project for the weekend, when most of us have a little more time to slow-roast the meat, then package portions for weeknight meals. The cooked meat keeps well in the freezer when wrapped securely in plastic or foil.

» Preheat the oven to 350 degrees F.

» Place the pork roast on a baking sheet that has been coated with cooking spray or lined with aluminum foil; sprinkle with salt and pepper. With a thin-bladed knife, cut small slits of various depths all over the roast. Insert 1 clove of garlic into each slit. Roast the pork until it is brown and very tender, about 2 hours. Cool. Shred the pork, discarding the bone and fat.

» Heat the oil in a large skillet over medium-high heat. Add the onions and sauté until tender, about 10 minutes. Add the shredded pork and cilantro; stir until heated through. Season with salt and pepper.

» Arrange warm tortillas on plates or a serving platter. Top each with pork and sprinkle with green onions. Serve with lime wedges and, if desired, salsa, sour cream, and chopped tomatoes.

Serves 4

1 bone-in pork shoulder, 3–4 pounds

Salt

Freshly ground black pepper

1 head garlic, cloves separated and peeled

2 tablespoons vegetable oil

2 large onions, chopped

1 cup chopped, fresh cilantro

12 corn tortillas, warmed

1 bunch green onions, chopped, green parts only

Lime wedges, for garnish

Salsa, sour cream, and chopped tomatoes, optional

WARMING TORTILLAS

Heat brings out the best flavor in all tortillas and makes them flexible enough to fold. Ideally, they should be warmed one by one over a burner flame or grill, flipping them very quickly several times with your fingertips or with tongs, which will give them a slight toastiness. A griddle or frying pan will also work, or an oven. About 10 seconds in a microwave will warm a flour tortilla, but corn tortillas dry out so quickly that they are best heated some other way. However you heat them, warm tortillas should be wrapped immediately in a cloth or foil and kept that way for serving. For larger quantities, wrap by the half dozen in foil packets and heat in a 350-degree oven for 10–15 minutes. Always be careful not to overheat and dry them out.

Fish Tacos with Citrus Slaw and Jalapeño-Lime Crema

Slaw

1 small head red cabbage, shredded

¼ cup fresh orange juice

Juice of ½ lime

2 tablespoons extra virgin olive oil

½ teaspoon salt

¼ teaspoon freshly ground black pepper

Crema

½ cup sour cream

½ cup mayonnaise

1 clove garlic, crushed

1 jalapeño, seeded and finely minced

Juice of one lime

Salt to taste

Ingredient list continued on following page

USE ANY FIRM WHITE FISH FOR THIS RECIPE, but be sure to check the Monterey Bay Aquarium's Seafood Watch list for the most sustainable and healthful options. Red cabbage gives the tacos crunch and color, jalapeños add a little heat, and the crema is cool and tangy. Who says healthful food doesn't taste good?

Slaw: Place the cabbage in a large bowl. In a smaller bowl, whisk together the orange juice, lime juice, and olive oil. Pour over the cabbage. Sprinkle with the salt and pepper and toss until cabbage is well coated with the dressing. Set aside at room temperature.

Crema: In a small bowl, whisk together the sour cream, mayonnaise, garlic, jalapeño, and lime juice. Sprinkle with salt and stir again. Taste and adjust seasoning, if necessary. Cover and refrigerate.

Fish: Rinse and pat dry the tilapia. In a small bowl, whisk together the olive oil, lime juice, cilantro, jalapeño, garlic, cumin, chile powder, salt, and pepper. Place the fish in a glass dish or zipper bag and then pour the marinade over, making sure all of the fish is coated. Set aside to marinate for at least 15 minutes, but no more than one hour.

» Heat the grill to high. Place the fish on a well-oiled grate or in a grilling basket. Turn after about 3 minutes and grill for another 2 minutes. Remove from heat, cover with foil and let sit while you warm the tortillas on the grill.

» To serve, shred the fish slightly with a fork. Place a serving of fish down the middle of each tortilla, then top with slaw and a drizzle of crema. Garnish with sliced avocado.

Serves 4

HOW TO BUY FISH AND SEAFOOD

Health experts have been saying for years that we need to replace the red meat in our diets with fish, and that's led to increased demand for the denizens of the deep. Unfortunately, that popularity has been accompanied by the exploitation and destruction of fisheries in oceans around the world. Many once-plentiful species are now threatened, including red snapper, orange roughy, and even anchovies.

The problem is complex and multi-faceted, but it is a result of several practices:

Overfishing. As demand has gone up, corporate fishing enterprises have grown and replaced smaller mom-and-pop-type fishermen, resulting in the mass extraction of vast numbers of fish without regard to the preservation of future stocks. Slow-growing, late-breeding species have suffered the most.

Piracy. Even in some well-regulated fisheries, piracy goes undetected and unpunished. Some experts estimate that a quarter of the world's catch is illegal.

Trawls, nets, and longlines. These practices destroy habitat critical to the health of the food chain and also result in bycatch, or the capture of unwanted and sometimes endangered species such as turtles, sharks, and seabirds.

Farming. Some farmed species are healthy and sustainable, such as oysters, mussels, tilapia, and some shrimp. But others, like farmed salmon, are raised in intensive operations that destroy natural habitat, spread disease, and result in a product with fewer health benefits than their wild-caught cousins.

None of this means you should avoid fish and seafood. By buying responsibly, you can support sustainable fishing practices and help avoid the further destruction of the ocean. Look for fish certified by the Marine Stewardship Council. Buy from a grocery store such as Whole Foods with educated fishmongers and a commitment to sustainable seafood. And get educated by visiting the Monterey Bay Aquarium's Seafood Watch website (montereybayaquarium.org/cr/seafoodwatch) or the Blue Ocean Institute (blueocean.org). Both offer guides to buying sustainable seafood, and the aquarium even has an app for your phone that will allow you to learn as you shop.

Fish

1½ pounds tilapia or other fish fillets

½ cup extra virgin olive oil

Juice of 3½ limes

½ cup fresh cilantro, finely chopped

1 jalapeño, seeded and finely minced

1 clove garlic, crushed

1 teaspoon ground cumin

1½ teaspoons chile powder

½ teaspoon salt

½ teaspoon pepper

12 corn tortillas

Sliced avocados for garnish

Carne Asada Tacos with Pico de Gallo

2 pounds top sirloin, cut across the grain into ⅛-inch slices

Juice of 6 limes

1 teaspoon garlic powder

2 tablespoons olive oil

8 small flour tortillas or gorditas

2 cups black beans, drained, and warmed

Pico de Gallo (page 52)

¼ cup pomegranate seeds

Easy Guacamole (page 58)

MOST MEXICAN COOKS USE SKIRT STEAK FOR CARNE ASADA, but top sirloin is generally easier to find and to handle. Keep the steak slightly frozen to make slicing easier. You can adjust the heat of the pico de gallo by increasing or decreasing the number of jalapeños. Pomegranate adds a touch of color and sweetness.

» Sprinkle the steak slices with the lime juice and garlic powder and toss to coat evenly, then allow them to sit at room temperature for 30 minutes. Heat the oil in a large skillet over high heat, then sear the sirloin slices about 30 seconds on each side until done.

» Warm the flour tortillas and beans. Stir the pomegranate seeds into the pico de gallo.

» Make do-it-yourself tacos with the tortillas, beans, meat, pico de gallo, and guacamole.

Serves 4

Chicken Enchiladas with Red Chile Sauce

4 boneless, skinless chicken breasts

Salt

Freshly ground black pepper

2 cups New Mexico Red Chile Sauce (page 46)

½ cup vegetable oil

1 dozen corn tortillas

¾ cup sliced green onions

1 cup sliced black olives

1 cup grated cheddar cheese

1 cup crumbled queso fresco

YOU CAN COOK THE CHICKEN FOR THIS DELICIOUS, comforting treat in advance, refrigerate for up to two days, and then make the enchiladas.

» Place the chicken breasts in a slow cooker. Season with salt and pepper. Cover with ¾ cup of the chile sauce. Reserve the remaining chile sauce. Cover and cook on low for 6 hours. Remove from slow cooker and shred the chicken.

» Alternatively, if you don't have a slow cooker, poach the chicken breasts in enough water to cover until they're fully cooked, about 25 minutes. Remove from the pan and shred. Return to the pan and add ¾ cup of chile sauce and simmer for 10–15 minutes.

» Preheat oven to 350 degrees F. Spray a 9 x 13-inch pan with cooking spray.

» In a small skillet, heat the vegetable oil over medium heat. In a small saucepan, heat the remaining chile sauce over low heat just until warm.

» One at a time, dip the corn tortillas into the hot oil until softened, about 5 seconds, and then into the chile sauce. Place in the prepared pan and top with a small amount of chicken, onions, olives, and cheddar. Roll and place seam-side-down in the pan. Repeat with the remaining tortillas, arranging the filled rolls to fit in the pan.

» Pour the remaining red chile sauce over the top of the enchiladas, then sprinkle with the cheddar and the queso fresco.

» Place in the oven for 25 minutes or until the cheese is melted. Remove from the oven and serve immediately, garnishing with the remaining green onions and olives.

Serves 4-6

Tortilla Soup

CHICKEN THIGHS ARE EXCELLENT for this classic recipe because they have more flavor than chicken breasts.

» In a large stockpot, heat the 2 tablespoons of corn oil. Sprinkle salt and pepper over the chicken and place the chicken in the pot. Sauté, meaty side down, about 2 minutes. Turn the chicken and add the onion, tomato, and garlic. Continue cooking about 2 more minutes.

» Add the stock. Bring the soup to a boil, then reduce the heat and simmer until the chicken is cooked through, about 15 minutes.

» Meanwhile, in a heavy skillet, fry the tortilla strips in the cup of corn oil until golden and crispy. Allow the tortilla strips to drain on a paper towel-lined plate.

» Remove the chicken thighs from the soup and, with two forks, separate the meat from the bones and discard the bones.

» Divide the chicken evenly among 6 bowls. Pour the broth over the chicken. Garnish with cilantro, lime juice, and the prepared tortilla strips.

Serves 6

1 cup corn oil, plus 2 tablespoons

Salt

Freshly ground black pepper

3 chicken thighs, bone-in, skinless

½ large onion, chopped

1 tomato, chopped and seeded

2 cloves garlic, finely chopped

6 cups high-quality, low-sodium chicken stock

3 corn tortillas, sliced into half-inch ribbons

2 tablespoons finely chopped fresh cilantro

2 tablespoons lime juice

Cheese Quesadillas

Cheese Quesadillas

4 medium flour tortillas

1 cup mild white cheese, grated

Salsa, pickled jalapeños, black olives, or other garnishes of your choice

ESSENTIALLY A GRILLED CHEESE SANDWICH with a Southwestern accent, the quesadilla is the perfect marriage of cheese (queso) and flatbread (tortilla). You can use your favorite cheese and either corn or flour tortillas. If you want to make more of a meal, you can also add shredded cooked chicken or beef. Experiment with your favorite ingredients to create your own tasty combinations, or try the unique variations below.

» Heat a large cast-iron skillet over medium-high heat. Lay one tortilla in the skillet and cover with half of the cheese. When the cheese starts to melt, cover with another tortilla, pressing it into the melting cheese. Gently turn with a spatula and cook the other side until the cheese is melted and the tortillas are browned.

Remove to a plate and cover to keep warm. Repeat the process with the remaining two tortillas and the rest of the cheese.

» Slice each quesadilla into six wedges and serve hot with your choice of garnishes on the side.

Serves 4

VARIATION
Squash Blossom Quesadillas

Squash Blossom Quesadillas

12 squash blossoms

½ pound asadero or other mild white cheese

½ cup chopped fresh cilantro

12 medium flour tortillas

WHEN YOUR SQUASH PLANTS HAVE an abundance of blossoms, pick about a dozen in the early morning and make quesadillas for lunch.

» Wash and dry the blossoms and tear each into 2 or 3 pieces. Follow the above directions for simple quesadillas, adding the squash blossoms and cilantro to the cheese on top of the tortillas. When they're browned and

the cheese is melted, slice into wedges and serve with your favorite salsa or other garnishes of your choice.

Serves 6

Roasted Garlic Quesadillas

THE MELLOW FLAVOR OF ROASTED GARLIC adds depth to this combination of chiles, onions, and mushrooms.

» Sauté the onion with a little oil until translucent; add mushrooms and continue to cook until just tender.

» Mix the onion/mushroom mixture with the chiles, garlic, and cheese in a medium-size bowl.

» Follow the directions for cheese quesadillas, spooning some of the vegetable-cheese mixture over the tortillas in the skillet and sprinkling with bacon, if desired. Top with another tortilla. Cook until the bottom tortillas begin to turn golden and the cheese starts to melt. Carefully turn over each quesadilla and cook a little longer, until the other side is also crisp and golden. Slide each quesadilla onto a cutting board and cut it into wedges. Serve hot with your favorite salsa.

Serves 6

1 small onion, diced

1 tablespoon olive or vegetable oil

½ pound mushrooms, sliced

2 roasted green chiles, julienned

1 head roasted garlic, removed from skins and mashed

½ pound mild white cheese, such as Oaxaca or Monterey Jack, grated

12 flour tortillas, about 8 inches each

6 strips bacon, chopped and cooked until crisp (optional)

Quick and Easy Chicken Avocado Fajitas

1–2 tablespoons olive oil

1 large yellow onion, cut into thin slices

4–6 cloves garlic, sliced very thin

2 boneless chicken breasts, cut into thin strips

Salt

Freshly ground black pepper

1 roasted bell pepper (page 32), seeded and julienned

1½ cups salsa (page 52)

2 avocados, thinly sliced

¼ cup chopped fresh cilantro

8–12 flour tortillas

Sour cream, for garnish

Fresh lime wedges, for garnish

ORIGINATING IN TEX-MEX COOKING, fajitas began as strips of grilled skirt steak wrapped in a flour tortilla. From that point the dish has expanded in many directions to include various meats, cheeses, vegetables, and flavorings. It's an informal treat, so each diner often assembles an individual serving by scooping up some of the mixture and rolling it in a flour tortilla. This version could be made vegetarian by omitting the chicken.

» Heat the olive oil in a large heavy skillet. Separate the onion into rings and gently sauté with the garlic until the onion is translucent. Add the chicken breasts and continue to sauté until the meat is opaque, letting it brown slightly around the edges. Season with salt and pepper. Add the roasted pepper and sauté just until heated through. Add the salsa, avocados, and cilantro, and continue to cook over moderate heat until heated through. Season to taste with more salt and pepper. Serve with fresh warm flour tortillas, and offer sour cream and lime wedges for garnish.

Serves 4–6

FRYING

Some iconic—and delicious—Southwestern dishes are fried. Fried foods, when done well, don't need to taste greasy, and if you use healthy fats, they won't make you unhealthy either. And remember, all things in moderation.

The first step is to use the right fat. Peanut oil, corn oil, grapeseed oil, and canola oil are all suitable. If you're going to use corn or canola oil, use organic versions if you want to avoid genetically modified products. Lard is the traditional fat for frying, and it's good, especially if you render it yourself from pasture-raised pork. (page 105)

The second concern is the size and type of pan. Use one big enough so that you can fry in batches without crowding. A large cast-iron skillet holds the temperature well and is deep enough for pan frying.

Step number three is to fry at the right temperature. For this you need a thermometer. Heat the oil or lard in a skillet to 350 degrees F for most foods. The oil should be shimmering, but not smoking. If it's smoking, it's too hot and more likely to catch fire. (And if it does, don't panic. Just cover the pan with a lid until the flames are out and then add more oil to cool it down.) If you don't have a thermometer, test the oil by dropping in a small piece of dough. It should sizzle and brown. If it just sits there, the oil isn't hot enough yet.

Finally, allow what you've just fried to drain well, first over the pan, and then on a bed of paper towels.

If you're concerned about what to do with the oil when you're finished, don't pour it down the sink to clog the drain. Cool it down, seal it in a container, and either recycle or dispose of it in the trash.

Carne Seca Chimichangas

CARNE SECA IS THE NAME GIVEN TO reconstituted dried beef (drying or "jerking" was a common pre-refrigeration method of meat preservation throughout the Southwest), cooked in onions, pepper, chile, and spices. The chimichanga was invented in Tucson, but by whom and when has always been in dispute. And really, does it matter? It's an institution in Southwest cuisine.

» Preheat oven to 325 degrees F.

» Puree the garlic in a blender with water until smooth. It should be thick and almost like a paste. If it's too thin and watery, drain some of the liquid. Toss the beef with puree and lime juice and spread evenly on a cookie sheet. Bake for 15 minutes until the meat dries out. The meat can be prepared to this point and then refrigerated for up to 3 days.

» Heat the olive oil in a large skillet and sauté the onion until transparent. Add the green chile, tomato, dried meat, and salt and pepper to taste. Mix well and heat through.

» Heat about two inches of oil in a large skillet to 350 degrees F.

» Heat the oven to 200 degrees F.

» Place a half cup of the meat mixture on a tortilla and roll into a burrito. Carefully slide into the hot oil. Brown on both sides, then remove to a plate covered with paper towels to drain. Place in the oven to keep warm while the others are cooking. Repeat seven times, making each burrito while the others fry so they don't get soggy.

» Garnish with grated cheese, lettuce, tomatoes and salsa, or serve smothered with red or green chile sauce (pages 46, 47).

Serves 8

---

16 cloves garlic, peeled

1 cup water

4 cups shredded cooked beef, such as brisket

¼ cup fresh lime juice

2 tablespoons olive oil

⅓ cup finely sliced onion

½ cup roasted, peeled, seeded, and chopped green chile

1 cup chopped fresh tomato

Salt

Freshly ground black pepper

8 large flour tortillas

1 cup oil, for frying

Grated cheese, shredded lettuce, chopped tomatoes, salsa, or red or green chile sauce, for garnish (optional)

Steak Burritos with Nopalitos

1 large *nopal* (page 27)

1 teaspoon olive oil

1½ pounds bottom round steak, 1 inch thick

Salt

Freshly ground black pepper

1 cup Mole Verde (page 50) or other salsa

4 large flour tortillas

2 cups cooked black beans (page 62)

1 cup crumbled cotija cheese

A CLASSIC BURRO OR BURRITO BEGINS WITH a large flour tortilla. It can contain a filling as modest as beans and cheese or as exotic as this intriguing combination. Fold top and bottom edges down over the filling, then roll the burrito sideways into a neat shape.

» Preheat the grill to medium high.

» Prepare the *nopal* and brush with olive oil. Place on the grill.

» Sprinkle the steak all over with salt and pepper, and put it on the grill. Cook the steak and *nopal* side-by-side, turning up to three times, until the meat is cooked to medium rare (page 75) and the *nopal* has turned from bright green to an olive color and is tender.

» Transfer the steak and the *nopal* to a cutting board. Cover the steak with foil and allow to rest while you cut the cactus into *nopalitos*, strips about the size of a green bean.

» In a small saucepan, heat the Mole Verde or other salsa.

» Thinly slice the beef.

» Warm the flour tortillas. Place a serving of black beans, steak, *nopalitos*, and ¼ cup of the Mole Verde on each tortilla. Sprinkle with cheese. Roll each into a burrito.

Serves 4

WHAT'S A NOPAL, AND WHY WOULD I WANT TO EAT ONE?

Nopales are the tender pads of the prickly pear cactus. They're best in the spring when they're young and not woody, and the spines haven't completely developed. They're nutritious—full of antioxidants, and they help regulate both blood sugar and serum cholesterol.

The flavor is mild and tart with a little bit of lemon, and the texture is crunchy, although when raw, they can be a little slimy. Cooking takes care of that, however. Nopales are used throughout the Southwest in salads and burritos, or as a condiment. They can be sliced (into nopalitos) and pickled.

If you don't have a prickly pear in your yard, you can usually find nopales at Mexican groceries. They're actually farmed in Mexico because they're such a popular vegetable. Choose pads that are large and tender. If they haven't been peeled (sometimes you can find them peeled, sliced, and ready to eat), then use a pair of tongs to hold the pad in place on a flat surface while you scrape it with a sharp knife. Be sure you remove all of the little tufts, called *glochids*, because they actually contain little barbed hairs. When you have the entire pad scraped clean, trim off the stem end and a margin all around, and rinse. The nopal is now ready to slice, stir-fry, roast, or grill.

Huevos Rancheros

1 cup mole verde, green chile, or other sauce

4 teaspoons bacon grease or unsalted butter, divided

4 corn tortillas

2 eggs

Salt

Freshly ground black pepper

½ small onion, chopped

½ cup shredded asadero cheese

SUNNY-SIDE UP OR OVER EASY, fried eggs will spill their warm, rich yolks into the sauce, which is what makes this dish so good. Use any salsa cocida (page 45) and serve with beans and additional warm tortillas on the side.

» In a small saucepan over low heat, gently warm the mole. If necessary, add enough water to reach the consistency of a thin cream soup.

» Add 1 teaspoon of the bacon grease to a cast-iron skillet over medium-low heat. Fry 1 tortilla on each side until warmed and softened. Transfer the tortilla to a plate. Repeat with the remaining grease and tortillas.

» In the same skillet, fry the eggs, seasoning with salt and pepper.

» On each serving plate, pour a dollop of the mole and top with a prepared tortilla. Pour more mole over it, top with another tortilla, and pour more mole over that, spreading it over the surface of the tortilla. Top with the fried eggs, garnish with onion and cheese, and serve immediately.

Serves 2

Migas

THIS SOUTHWESTERN BREAKFAST dish makes good use of leftover tortilla chips.

» In a heavy skillet, melt the butter. Add the tortilla chips, onion, bell pepper, and green chiles, and sauté until the onion is softened.

» Add the eggs and cilantro, and cook, stirring well, until the eggs are mostly done. Add the chorizo and cook 2 minutes longer. Remove from heat. Serve garnished with Pico de Gallo.

Serves 4–6

Chilaquiles

THIS IS AN EASY AND THRIFTY WAY to use up corn tortillas that have passed their prime. Serve it for breakfast or brunch with a side of fried or scrambled eggs and refried beans. You can also use green chile or mole in place of the red chile sauce. If you're feeding a crowd for brunch, this is an easy recipe to expand.

» Pour the vegetable oil into a large skillet over medium-high heat. Fry the tortillas in the hot oil until browned, then remove from the skillet and drain on paper towels.

» When all of the tortillas are cooked, add the chile sauce to the pan and heat to bubbling. Add the tortillas and turn to make sure each piece is coated with sauce. Allow to simmer for a few minutes more.

» Plate the mixture and top with cheese, jalapeño, cilantro, and avocado.

Serves 2

Migas

3 tablespoons butter

24 corn tortilla chips

½ cup diced onion

½ cup diced red bell pepper

½ cup roasted, peeled, and diced green chiles (page 32)

12 eggs, lightly beaten

¼ cup finely chopped fresh cilantro

½ pound chorizo, cooked and drained (page 84)

1 cup Pico de Gallo (page 52)

Chilaquiles

2 tablespoons vegetable oil

6 corn tortillas, cut into wedges

1 cup New Mexico Red Chile Sauce (page 46)

½ cup crumbled cotija cheese

1 jalapeño, stemmed, seeded, and chopped (optional)

¼ cup chopped fresh cilantro

1 avocado, chopped

CHILES

CHILES—FROM THE MILD ANAHEIM TO THE FIERY HOT HABANERO to the tiny, incendiary chiltepín—have been a staple of cooking in the American Southwest, Mexico, Central and South America, and the Caribbean for almost as long as people have lived in those parts of the world. The first peppers must have been gathered wild, but soon they were domesticated. Chiles, corn, and tomatoes remain signature flavors of New World cuisine, and chiles sing the loudest and most memorably.

Chiles in their grassy, lively, green form can be found in appetizers, soups, stews, salsas, and casseroles. In their sweet, ripe, red form, they dry and store well and can be ground into powder and turned into sauces that light up the flavor of anything they touch. It's easy to find canned green chiles in almost every supermarket, but the flavor of fresh roasted chiles can't be beat. Buy a big batch when they're in season, roast them (page 32), and store them in the freezer so you'll have them during the long months of winter.

Roasted Green Chiles

5 pounds green chiles

ONE OF THE BEST THINGS ABOUT LIVING IN THE SOUTHWEST is the scent of roasting chiles that permeates the air on street corners and at farmers markets in late August and September. It's easy to do it yourself, and the smell is just as wonderful.

» To do a large batch, preheat the grill to high. Wash and dry the chiles and then lay them on the grill. Using a long pair of tongs, turn the chiles frequently so that they become blackened and blistered all over. Place the roasted chiles in a large bowl and cover with plastic wrap to allow the skin to loosen. Set aside for 10 to 15 minutes.

» Remove the chiles from the bowl and peel off the skins with your fingers. You can also remove the seeds, if you so desire. Avoid running water over the chiles as you peel and seed them because that also rinses away the volatile oils that contain much of the flavor.

» Use immediately, or freeze in small quantities for use later.

» For a smaller batch, roast them under the broiler in the oven or over a gas flame.

HOW TO HANDLE CHILES

Few things are more painful than touching a sensitive body part, like your eyes, after seeding and chopping hot green chiles. Some people have been known to suffer burning fingers and hands for hours after making a batch of salsa. That's why it's always best to wear disposable food service gloves when you're working with jalapeños, habaneros, or other spicy varieties. Capsaicin, the oil that makes the heat, permeates the flesh of the chile, but is most prominent in the seeds and ribs inside. If you do get it on your hands, the best way to get rid of it is to wash thoroughly with lots of soap and water, and then avoid scratching your nose or rubbing your eyes for several hours afterward. There are plenty of old wives' tales about rinsing with lemon juice or vinegar or dipping your hands in milk, but really, soap and water is the most effective.

Chipotles en Adobo

CHIPOTLES ARE SMOKED AND DRIED JALAPEÑOS and can be used to give almost any dish a smoky flavor. If you like to garden and you find yourself with a bumper crop of jalapeños, leave them on the plant until they turn red, then harvest and make your own chipotles. You can also use the green peppers. Once they're dried, the chipotles can be stored in an airtight jar or bag, or added to adobo sauce, a spicy condiment used in sauces and main dishes.

» Wash the jalapeños and discard any that have blemishes or soft spots. Remove the stems and make a small slit in the side of each one.

» Soak the wood in water for at least 1 hour. Prepare the smoker or grill and bring the heat to 200 degrees F.

» Place the peppers in a single layer on the top rack in the smoker, farthest away from the heat. If the peppers are too small for the rack, cut a piece of wire mesh to fit and place it on the rack underneath the peppers. Cover and allow to smoke for 3–5 hours or until the peppers are shriveled and pliable. Stir about once an hour and make sure that the temperature and smoke stay constant.

» The smoked peppers will still contain a small amount of moisture. To dry completely, use a food dehydrator or place on the rack in an oven at very low temperature until the peppers are brown and hard.

» At this point they may be stored for up to six months or ground in a food processor to make chipotle powder. Be sure to wear a mask and avoid inhaling the pungent dust.

» To make the adobo sauce, combine about 12 chipotles, the water, onion, vinegar, ketchup, garlic, cumin, oregano, and salt in a heavy saucepan. Simmer over low heat for 1–2 hours until the chipotles are soft and the sauce is reduced to about a cup. Refrigerate for up to six weeks or freeze for up to three months.

Makes ½ pound of dried chipotles, or 2 cups of chipotles en adobo

5 pounds red jalapeños

Hickory, pecan, or other hardwood chips or chunks

4 cups water

½ cup dried onion

½ cup cider vinegar

¼ cup ketchup

3 cloves garlic, minced

¼ teaspoon ground cumin

¼ teaspoon dried oregano

¼ teaspoon salt

Garlic Cheese-Stuffed Jalapeño Peppers

12 large fresh jalapeños

6 cloves garlic, minced

⅓ cup minced red onion

¼ cup minced red bell pepper

¼ cup cream cheese

¼ cup shredded Oaxaca cheese (or substitute Monterey Jack)

½ pound thick-sliced bacon, each piece cut in half

½ cup crema (Mexican-style sour cream, or substitute crème fraîche or regular sour cream)

IT'S SURPRISING HOW MANY PEOPLE who say they don't eat jalapeños will devour a few of these tasty bites. Perfect for an appetizer served with a frosty margarita or ice-cold cerveza. In the summer, try cooking these on the grill.

» Line a sheet pan with aluminum foil or parchment.

» Slice off the stem ends of the jalapeños and scoop out the seeds, creating hollows for the stuffing.

» Mix the garlic, onion, bell pepper, and cheeses in a small bowl. Stuff each jalapeño with the cheese mixture and wrap it with a piece of bacon, securing with two toothpicks.

» Turn on the broiler in the oven. Broil the bacon-wrapped peppers for about 10-15 minutes, then remove them from the oven and turn each one over. Return to the broiler for another 8 minutes or so, until the bacon is browned.

» Serve immediately, drizzled with a bit of crema.

Serves 6

Green Chile Eggs Benny

2 cups cooked black beans, drained (page 62)

2 scallions, sliced thin (white and green parts)

1 jalapeño, seeds and ribs removed, diced

1 tomato, seeded and diced

1 tablespoon lime juice

Salt

Freshly ground black pepper

1 cup Mexican *crema* (or substitute crème fraîche or regular sour cream)

2 roasted poblano chiles, peeled, seeds and stems removed, and diced

Zest of one lime

1 teaspoon red chile powder

8 large eggs, poached

4 English muffins, toasted

8 slices of ham, optional

2 tablespoons chopped chives, for garnish

4 lime wedges, for garnish

EGGS BENEDICT WITH A SOUTHWESTERN TWIST, this is a crowd pleaser for family Sunday brunch. Halved, it's also the perfect festive meal for two.

» In a medium saucepan, combine the beans, scallions, jalapeño, tomato, and lime juice. Heat over medium-high heat; simmer for 5 minutes until the beans are heated through. Season with salt and pepper. Reduce heat and keep warm.

» In a medium mixing bowl, combine the *crema*, poblanos, lime zest, and chile powder. Season with salt and pepper. Allow to sit for 10 minutes or longer before serving.

» Poach the eggs and toast the English muffins. On each of 4 plates, lay 2 English muffin halves topped with a slice of ham (optional). Ladle 2–3 tablespoons of black bean mixture over each muffin half. Gently place a poached egg over the beans. Spoon 1 tablespoon of the *crema* mixture over each egg, and garnish with chopped chives and a lime wedge.

Serves 4

Gazpacho

DON'T BE TEMPTED TO MAKE THIS SOUP when you can't find perfectly ripe tomatoes. It's not worth even the minimal effort of making it. But when tomatoes are bountiful and sweet, there's no better use for them.

» In a blender or food processor, process the tomatoes, cucumbers, onion, and bell peppers until blended but still slightly chunky. Do not puree.

» Pour the mixture into a large glass pitcher. Stir in the lime juice, garlic, jalapeños, and cilantro. Season with salt and pepper to taste.

» Chill for at least 1 hour to allow the flavors to blend. Serve with warm, crusty bread.

Serves 8

2½ pounds perfectly ripe tomatoes

2 medium cucumbers, peeled and seeded

1 large red onion, coarsely chopped

2 red, yellow, or orange bell peppers, seeded and coarsely chopped

Juice of 2 limes or lemons

3 cloves garlic, finely chopped

2 jalapeños, seeded and finely chopped

¼ cup finely chopped fresh cilantro

Salt

Freshly ground black pepper

8 pieces warm, crusty bread

Chile and Cheese Avocado Soup

2 tablespoons olive oil

1 medium-size yellow onion, sliced into thin rings

4–6 cloves garlic, minced

1 small jalapeño, seeded and cut into thin rings

6 cups chicken broth

1 cup fresh salsa

2 large avocados, diced

¼ cup chopped cilantro

Salt

Freshly ground black pepper

1 cup grated extra-sharp cheddar cheese

1 cup ricotta cheese, crumbled

Cilantro sprigs, for garnish

Lime wedges, for garnish

AVOCADOS ARE YET ANOTHER NATIVE AMERICAN GIFT to gastronomy. Rich and satisfying, this soup can make a meal when served with fresh warm bread or tortillas.

» Heat the olive oil in a heavy skillet over moderate heat and gently sauté the onion rings, garlic, and jalapeño until the onion is soft and translucent and just beginning to brown.

» Place in a large pot with the broth and salsa and bring to a boil. Remove from heat and stir in the avocado and cilantro. Season to taste with salt and pepper. Ladle into serving bowls and sprinkle cheddar and ricotta cheeses over the top. Garnish each bowl with a sprig of fresh cilantro and a wedge of lime.

Serves 4–6

Green Chile Stew

GREEN CHILE STEW IS A NEW MEXICAN TRADITION, and it goes with everything. Nothing is better in the depths of winter than a big bowl of green chile stew with a soft, warm flour tortilla on the side.

» In a large stockpot, heat the olive oil until shimmering. While it's heating, dredge the pork cubes in a mixture of flour, ½ teaspoon salt, and ¼ teaspoon pepper. Add the cubes to the hot oil in batches so that they're not crowded in the pot. Allow to brown on all sides and then remove from the pot.

» When all of the pork is browned, add the onions and garlic to the pot. Stir for about 5 minutes until soft. Add the tomatoes and deglaze the bottom of the pot. Return the pork to the pot and add the jalapeño, green chiles, and stock. Bring to a boil and then cover the pot and reduce heat to simmer. Cook for an hour. Taste the stew and add 2 teaspoons salt and 1 teaspoon pepper to taste. Simmer for another half hour until the meat is completely tender.

» Serve with flour tortillas, or pour over burritos, enchiladas, tamales, or scrambled eggs.

Serves 8

2 tablespoons extra virgin olive oil

3 pounds boneless pork shoulder, trimmed and cut into 1-inch cubes

½ cup all purpose flour

2½ teaspoons salt, divided

1¼ teaspoon freshly ground black pepper, divided

1 medium yellow onion, diced

4 cloves garlic, minced

1 can (28-ounce) fire-roasted diced tomatoes

1 jalapeño, seeded and diced

2½ cups roasted, peeled, and seeded green chiles, chopped

1 quart chicken stock

Cazuela

2 tablespoons extra virgin olive oil

2 pounds stew meat

2 teaspoons salt, divided

1½ teaspoons freshly ground black pepper, divided

2 tablespoons all-purpose flour

1 medium onion, finely diced

4 cloves garlic, finely minced

1½ cups tomato sauce

5 poblano chiles, roasted, peeled, seeded, and coarsely chopped

1 quart beef stock

½ cup fresh cilantro, finely chopped

A CAZUELA, OR CASSEROLE, IS A CLAY COOKING DISH, and it's also a stew prepared with squash and other vegetables and meats. This Mexican version is based on a recipe that comes from an old cookbook of traditional foods eaten throughout the Southwest. Resist the urge to add a bunch of spices or other vegetables—the beauty is in the simplicity. If you have fresh lard, use it; otherwise, use olive or organic canola oil.

» In a heavy stockpot, heat the oil. Pat dry the cubes of stew meat and sprinkle with 1 teaspoon salt and 1 teaspoon pepper. When the oil is hot, add the cubes in small batches of a few at a time, turning until browned on all sides. Remove to a plate.

» If there's not at least two tablespoons of oil remaining in the pot, add more and let it get hot. Sprinkle the flour over the hot oil. Stir constantly until the flour is a little bit lighter than the color of peanut butter, about 15 minutes. Add the onion and garlic and continue stirring until the onions are translucent. Stir in the tomato sauce and chiles. Add the beef stock and cilantro, and then add the browned beef.

» Season with remaining salt and pepper, bring to a boil, and then cover and reduce heat to keep the liquid at a simmer. Cover and cook about an hour, until the beef is tender. Uncover and let cook another ten minutes to thicken the gravy.

» Serve with flour tortillas.

Serves 6

Chiles Rellenos

RELLENO MEANS "FILLED" OR "STUFFED" IN SPANISH. These chiles rellenos are full of flavor and as crispy as a quick dip in the frying pan will provide. The trick to fast dipping is to dry the chiles well enough so that the batter will stick to them. To make them hold together well, it is also helpful to chill the stuffed chiles before dipping and frying them. You can substitute canned whole green chiles, which will not have stems.

» Spray or oil a 9 x 13-inch baking dish. Heat oven to 325 degrees F.

» Clean the seeds from inside the chiles and pat dry. Carefully slice about an inch lengthwise into each whole chile just below the stem. Insert a stick of cheese into each chile, or fill with grated cheese, and place the pods into a shallow pan, large enough to hold all 12 chiles.

» Place the prepared baking pan into the oven to heat it slightly before putting the battered chiles into it.

» Beat the egg whites in a medium-size mixing bowl on high speed until stiff. Fold in the separately beaten yolks and then the flour and salt. Pour the batter over the chiles, carefully turning the chiles to coat evenly. (Leave the stems intact.) Heat enough oil in a large frying pan to cover the chiles. Meanwhile, carefully remove the baking dish from the oven and set it on a heat-safe area next to the frying pan.

» Using a long-slotted spatula, dip each relleno into the hot oil just long enough to cook the egg batter and then transfer it into the heated baking dish. When all the rellenos are in the baking dish, bake them in the preheated oven for 25 minutes or until golden brown. Remove from the oven and serve immediately.

» Rellenos go well with the old-fashioned favorites: *quelites* (wild greens) and beans, Spanish rice (page 70), and fresh sliced tomatoes. They are also good topped with salsa or New Mexico Green Chile Sauce (page 47).

Serves 6

12 long green chiles, roasted and peeled but with the stems in place, if possible

¾ pound longhorn cheddar cheese, cut into one-ounce sticks, or an equal amount grated

4 eggs, separated

2 tablespoons flour

½ teaspoon salt

Oil for frying

Wild Mushroom and Roasted Poblano Empanadas

2 tablespoons butter

2 cups masa harina (page 8)

1 teaspoon salt

1 cup vegetable stock or water

2 tablespoons fresh lard or vegetable oil

2 fresh poblano chiles, roasted, peeled, seeded, and chopped

½ pound wild mushrooms, brushed clean and chopped

1 teaspoon minced garlic

Salt

Freshly ground black pepper

1½ cups crumbled *cotija* cheese (page 4)

2 cups Mole Verde (page 50)

THESE ARE LIKE QUESADILLAS made with small corn tortillas. Use whatever kind of wild mushrooms you can find in your market, such as a combination of chanterelles, oyster mushrooms, and morels. Don't be put off by the high price per pound of wild mushrooms because just a few go a long way. Or substitute cultivated mushrooms, mixing more than one type, if possible, for extra flavor.

» In a large mixing bowl, work the butter into the masa harina and salt, using a pastry blender or your hands. Add the vegetable stock or water and work into a firm dough. Divide the dough into 4 quarters. From each of the quarters roll 3 cherry tomato-sized balls.

» In a cast-iron skillet over medium heat, melt the lard or oil and sauté the poblanos, mushrooms, and garlic together until the mushrooms release their juices. Remove from the heat and season to taste with salt and pepper.

» Flatten the dough balls into 6-inch discs using a tortilla press or a rolling pin. (Putting each ball between two pieces of wax paper will help prevent sticking.)

» Heat a cast-iron skillet or *comal* over medium heat. First, place a tortilla on the comal and cook for one minute. Flip the tortilla and arrange on half of it 2 tablespoons of the mushroom mixture and about 2 tablespoons of the cheese. Fold the other half over and use a fork to press the edges together, sealing it shut. Cook for about 3 minutes on each side, or until golden. Repeat with the remaining ingredients.

» Serve the empanadas drizzled with Mole Verde.

Makes 12

Carne Asada Sandwiches

YOU WILL NEVER LOOK AT LUNCHTIME in the same blasé way after you experience one of these sandwiches! For this outstanding recipe you will need a grill.

» Mix the canola oil, lime juice, chile de árbol, black pepper, and garlic with the beef in a gallon-size zip-top bag. Place the bag in a bowl in the refrigerator, and allow the meat to marinate for 1 to 24 hours.

» Make the sandwich spread: mix the mayonnaise with the lime zest and hot sauce to taste.

» Heat a grill or stove-top grill pan to high.

» Drizzle the onion slices with the olive oil, season with salt and pepper, then place on the grill for 4 minutes per side. Remove the steak from the marinade; discard the marinade. Season the steak with salt and pepper, then grill for approximately 3–5 minutes per side, to the desired degree of doneness. Remove from the grill and cover with foil to allow the steak to rest for 10 minutes. Slice thinly across the grain.

» Assemble the sandwiches on the focaccia with the spread, sliced steak, roasted pepper and chile, grilled onion, and avocado slices, as desired.

2 servings

2 tablespoons canola oil

1 tablespoon lime juice (or other fruit juice)

1 chile de árbol, split

¼ teaspoon freshly ground black pepper

1 clove garlic, roughly chopped

½ pound chuck, sirloin, or round steak

2 tablespoons mayonnaise

Zest of 1 lime

Tabasco or other favorite bottled hot sauce

2 thick slices red onion

1 tablespoon olive oil

Salt

Freshly ground black pepper

2 squares focaccia (5 inches each), or other hearty sandwich bread or roll, split

1 large red bell pepper, roasted, peeled, seeded, and cut into one-inch chunks

1 poblano, roasted, peeled, seeded, and cut into one-inch chunks

1 ripe avocado, peeled, pitted, and sliced

SALSAS & SAUCES

SALSAS COCIDAS (COOKED SAUCES) ARE ONE OF THE BASIC building blocks of Southwest cooking. From simple red and green sauces to complex moles and delicate cream sauces, *salsas cocidas* add depth and flavor to almost any meat, fish, or vegetarian dish. They make an excellent braising sauce for poultry and pork, and it's not unusual to find them garnishing—or smothering—burritos, eggs, and tamales throughout the Southwest.

Red chile-based sauces tend to have an earthy, spicy flavor profile, while green sauces are usually a little on the lighter, brighter side with a more sharply vegetal taste. Either version can be as hot as you want to make it, depending on the type of chiles you use. If you're feeling festive, you can smother your burrito with both. In the Southwest, that's known as Christmas style.

Most grocery stores carry canned or bottled sauces, but it's easy to make your own. They freeze well, so you can make a big batch and always have some on hand for when the mood strikes. Once you've mastered the techniques, you can get creative at any meal of the day.

Salsas crudas (fresh, uncooked sauces) are frequently served as a condiment in the Southwest. While the most traditional recipes use some combination of tomatoes, peppers, onion, and garlic, you can also make a salsa from almost any combination of fruits and vegetables. Your own fresh salsa, even the simplest one, will taste miraculously better than the store-bought kind. It takes only a few common ingredients and a few moments of chopping.

New Mexico Red Chile Sauce

24 dried red New Mexico chiles

4 cups beef stock, chicken stock, or water

2 tablespoons bacon grease, lard, or vegetable oil

2 cloves garlic, minced

2 tablespoons flour

1 teaspoon dried Mexican oregano

Salt

Honey (optional)

HERE IS A VERSION OF NEW MEXICO'S famous red chile sauce. Mixed with shredded pork, it is used as a tamale filling, but all by itself it is also ladled over tamales as well as enchiladas, huevos rancheros, breakfast burritos, stuffed sopaipillas, chiles rellenos, and almost anything else you can think of. You may not need 4 cups of the sauce for your recipe, but you might as well make the whole batch. Freeze extra portions in small resealable plastic containers for later use.

» In a large cast-iron skillet over medium heat, toast the chiles on both sides (you'll have to do this in batches) until they soften slightly and become aromatic. When the chiles are cool enough to handle, remove the stems and seeds.

» Transfer the chiles to a deep saucepan and pour the stock or water over them. Bring the mixture to a boil, then reduce the heat and simmer for about 10 minutes. Remove the pan from the heat and allow the chiles to rest, about 15 minutes.

» Working in batches, puree the chiles with their soaking liquid.

» In the cast-iron skillet over medium heat, melt the bacon grease. Add the garlic and flour and cook, stirring until the mixture becomes golden. Add the pureed chiles and stir quickly while the sauce bubbles and spatters. Reduce the heat, add the oregano, and simmer for 5 minutes. Season to taste with salt. If the sauce is a little bitter, mellow it with about a teaspoon of honey to taste.

Makes about 4 cups

New Mexico Green Chile Sauce

THIS IS PROBABLY NEW MEXICO'S MOST FAMOUS RECIPE; it's one that visitors to the state always remember. The sauce is best made with freshly roasted chiles, but you can also use canned or frozen chiles. Pour leftover sauce over eggs, enchiladas, burritos, or tacos.

» In a skillet over medium heat, sauté the onion and garlic in the lard until soft.

» Sprinkle the flour over the onion mixture and cook, stirring, until the flour becomes golden. Whisking constantly, pour in the chicken stock and continue whisking until it is completely incorporated.

» Add the chiles, tomato, and salt, then reduce the heat and simmer about 15 minutes. Serve warm.

Makes about 2 ½ cups

New Mexico Green Chile Sauce

1 small white onion, chopped

2 cloves garlic, minced

2 tablespoons lard or oil

1 tablespoon all-purpose flour

2 cups homemade or low-sodium chicken stock

1 cup chopped roasted New Mexico chiles, peeled, stemmed, and seeded (page 2)

1 small tomato, peeled and chopped

1 teaspoon salt, or to taste

Smoky Chipotle Salsa Roja

IF YOUR TAMALES TURN OUT DRIER than you had expected, you can throw this salsa together in a flash and your guests will swoon with joy. It's also good on chiles rellenos, burritos, or huevos rancheros.

» Heat the lard in a heavy-bottomed saucepan over medium heat and add the onion, garlic, tomatoes, and chipotles. Fry the mixture, stirring constantly, for 5–10 minutes, until the sauce has thickened. Season to taste with salt and serve warm.

Makes about 2 ½ cups

Smoky Chipotle Salsa Roja

1 tablespoon lard or vegetable oil

½ cup diced white onion

1 clove garlic, minced

1 can (15-ounce) crushed tomatoes

2 chipotles in adobo, minced (page 33)

Salt

CHOCOLATE

The story of chocolate is full of surprises. Who first tried to eat the bitter seeds of a bizarre, bloated tropical fruit, now called cacao? To be edible, those bean-like seeds require fermentation, roasting, grinding, and flavoring, so we must give the residents of Honduras some 3,500 years ago three cheers for their great persistence and ingenuity.

Once processed, chocolate revealed its delightful flavor and mild health- and mood-enhancing side effects. It became a pre-Columbian treasure: a symbol of power, a form of currency, a magic potion, and even part of the last rites before human sacrifice. Chocolate was commonly mixed with chile and corn, and sometimes with even more potent substances, such as hallucinogens. Probably chocolate also found its way into sauces such as mole, but for most of its history it was served mainly as a frothy beverage. It was a special treat, but it was not sweet.

In this form, chocolate first came to the Southwest more than 1,000 years ago. Traces have been identified on pottery from Utah that dates from the 800s, and also detected on unusual clay beakers used at Chaco Canyon, New Mexico, in the 1200s. The precious tropical beans must have been carried to the desert from far away in the south, perhaps to trade for turquoise and copper. Probably this early Southwestern chocolate drink was used only in religious rituals, but we really do not know.

We do know that chocolate was one of Columbus's earliest and most important discoveries. When Spanish ships sailed home laden with booty, the new food that first became fashionable in Europe was not chile, corn, or tomatoes—but chocolate. Although Europeans promptly sweetened it, and they liked to drink it hot, chocolate was prepared in more or less the same way until the onset of the Industrial Revolution, when for the first time in 3,000 years, new technological breakthroughs began to occur. Soon, mechanical processes were developed that led to cheaper, more widely available drinking chocolate, and then to chocolate candy.

Since then, chocolate has become a common household item. Besides being made into brownies and bunnies, it has gone to war, to the tops of the highest mountains, and into space. Its nutritional properties have been extensively analyzed. It has taken many new forms, both sweet and savory. And recently, chocolate has reunited with its old friend chile to create surprising, delicious, and truly essential Southwestern recipes, some of which you will find in these pages.

Mole Poblano

THIS VERSION IS ADAPTED FROM THE SPICY FOOD LOVER'S BIBLE *by Nancy Gerlach and Dave DeWitt, who is affectionately known as the Pope of Peppers. Mole poblano comes from the Mexican state of Puebla (hence the name poblano) but as the most famous and most beloved sauce in Mexico, it is served almost everywhere. There are many stories about its creation, but most of them give credit to a seventeenth-century nun, Sister Andrea, who invented the dish in the kitchen of the convent of Santa Cruz. It is a marvelous blend of local ingredients (chile, chocolate, turkey) with ones introduced from Europe (almonds, sesame seed, lard). This mole is traditionally served with poached turkey, which is simmered in the sauce for the last 30 minutes of cooking time. It is delicious with chicken as well.*

» In a cast-iron skillet over medium heat, toast the ancho and New Mexico chiles on both sides until they soften slightly and become aromatic. Transfer to a medium, heat-proof bowl and pour in enough hot water to cover. Keep the chiles submerged with a small plate or saucer for 15 minutes. Drain the chiles and discard the water.

» Put the rehydrated chiles, chipotles, onion, garlic, tomatoes, 2 tablespoons of sesame seeds, almonds, tortilla, raisins, cloves, cinnamon, and coriander in the blender. Puree the mixture, and, with the motor running, slowly add enough stock to form a smooth sauce.

» Heat the lard in a large, heavy saucepan over medium heat. When it's hot enough to shimmer, add the sauce and simmer for 10 minutes, stirring frequently. Add more stock to the sauce to keep it smooth and to thin it if it gets too thick. Reduce heat, stir in the chocolate, and cook over very low heat for 30 minutes or until the sauce has thickened. Season to taste with salt and pepper. Serve garnished with the remaining sesame seeds.

Makes about 6 cups

---

4 dried ancho chiles, stemmed and seeded

8 dried red New Mexico chiles, stemmed and seeded

2 chipotles in adobo (page 33)

2 cups chopped onion

4 cloves garlic, minced

4 medium tomatoes, chopped

¼ cup sesame seeds, divided

1 cup toasted almonds, chopped

½ corn tortilla, torn into pieces

½ cup raisins

½ teaspoon ground cloves

¼ teaspoon ground cinnamon

¼ teaspoon ground coriander

4–6 cups chicken or turkey stock

3 tablespoons lard or vegetable oil

2 ounces bittersweet chocolate

Salt

Freshly ground black pepper

Mole Verde

THIS GREEN MOLE, A SMOOTH, SUBTLE SAUCE, is made with pepitas (roasted and hulled pumpkin seeds—look for them in the bulk aisle of your natural foods store). Versatile mole verde tastes great over chicken, pork, fish, and even steak.

¾ pound tomatillos, husked and washed

3 cups chicken stock

1 cup pepitas

¼ teaspoon cumin seeds

4 whole cloves

3-inch piece of canela (cinnamon)

2 jalapeños, stemmed, seeded, and chopped

1 poblano, stemmed, seeded, and roughly chopped

½ medium onion, roughly chopped

2 cloves garlic

1 tablespoon vegetable oil

1 cup fresh cilantro leaves, washed and dried

3 romaine lettuce leaves, washed and dried

» Put the tomatillos and stock in a medium saucepan, bring to a boil, reduce heat, and simmer 15 minutes.

» Meanwhile, in a cast-iron skillet over medium heat, toast the pepitas, cumin seeds, cloves, and canela until the seeds start to pop and turn golden. Transfer the seeds and spices to a blender and puree with about 1 cup of the stock from the tomatillo pot. With a rubber spatula, scrape the puree into a small bowl and set aside.

» When the tomatillos are done, drain and reserve the stock. Transfer the tomatillos to the empty blender. Add the jalapeños and poblano, onion, and garlic and puree until smooth, adding a little stock if necessary. Scrape the puree into a large bowl.

» In the same skillet over medium heat, fry the pumpkin seed mixture in the oil until it browns slightly.

» Meanwhile, add the cilantro and lettuce leaves to the blender and puree with 1 cup of the stock. Add the pureed leaves and the tomatillo mixture to the skillet and heat through. Serve immediately.

Makes about 3 cups

Garlic Chile con Queso

THIS QUESO IS RIGHT AT HOME when served with crisp tortilla chips or as the sauce for a pan of enchiladas. Try a variety of cheeses to come up with the combination you like best. Just avoid the processed orange stuff!

» Heat a saucepan over medium to medium-high heat and add the oil. When the oil shimmers, add the onion and garlic and sauté until soft and translucent.

» Add the jalapeños and tomatoes. Turn the heat down to low and add grated cheddar and Monterey Jack cheeses, stirring until melted. Add sour cream and stir well. Do not allow the mixture to boil. When it is warmed through, remove from heat and serve.

» Serving tip: keep warm in a slow cooker set on low heat.

Serves 6–8

1 tablespoon olive or vegetable oil

1 cup finely chopped white or yellow onion

6 cloves garlic, finely minced

1–2 fresh jalapeños, stemmed, seeded, and finely chopped

1 can chopped tomatoes (14½-ounce), drained

8 ounces cheddar cheese, grated

8 ounces Monterey Jack cheese, grated

1 cup sour cream

Pico de Gallo

PICO DE GALLO, THE MOST COMMON SALSA in Mexico, is quick and easy and goes well with almost anything. Use it to top eggs, steaks, and tacos, or simply serve it with tortilla chips.

» In a bowl, combine the tomatoes, onion, jalapeños, and cilantro. Add the lime juice and salt to taste. Allow the mixture to sit at room temperature for about 30 minutes to let the flavors fully develop.

Makes about 3 cups

Salsa de Molcajete

IMPRESS YOUR GUESTS by making this traditional salsa with a big lava-rock mortar and pestle (molcajete and tejolote). If you don't have one, put the ingredients in the work bowl of your food processor and pulse until it is blended but still chunky. Serve the salsa in the molcajete with freshly fried tortilla chips (page 10). If you prefer green salsa rather than red, substitute tomatillos for the tomatoes.

» Using the tejolote, grind the garlic to a paste in the molcajete. Add the onion and jalapeños and grind until blended. Add the tomatoes, crushing and grinding until blended but still chunky. Season to taste with salt.

Makes about 1 ½ cups

VARIATION
Salsa Verde de Molcajete

» Replace the tomatoes with ½ pound tomatillos, husked and chopped, and add 2 tablespoons chopped fresh cilantro leaves.

Makes about 1.5 cups

PICO DE GALLO

Fresh Corn Salsa

2 cooked, cooled, and shucked ears of corn

1 medium tomato, finely diced

½ small red onion, finely chopped

1 jalapeño, stemmed, seeded, and minced

2 tablespoons minced fresh cilantro, basil, or tarragon

Juice of 1 lime

Salt

IT'S EASY TO OVERESTIMATE the amount of fresh corn to buy for a backyard barbecue. No problem: just make this marvelous, chewy salsa with the leftovers.

» Stand an ear of corn upright on a cutting board and slice off the kernels. Run the knife down the cob afterward to scrape out all of the little milky bits. Repeat with the other ear and transfer the corn to a medium bowl.

» Toss the corn with the tomato, onion, jalapeño, cilantro, and lime juice. Season to taste with salt.

Makes about 2 cups

Tomato Soup with Fresh Corn Salsa and Chipotle Cream

MAKE THIS SIMPLE SOUP in the summer when local tomatoes are plentiful and inexpensive. By not boiling the tomatoes, you can preserve their fresh flavor. One big batch will last a week in the refrigerator and can be served with a number of different garnishes. If you're rushed, decorate each bowl with fresh cilantro. If you have a little more time, try these pretty, complementary garnishes.

» In a stainless steel or enameled cast-iron stockpot, combine the olive oil, tomatoes, cilantro, and garlic. Do not bring to a boil, but cook over medium-low heat until the tomatoes soften, about 20 minutes.

» Over a large bowl, press the tomato mixture through a mesh strainer to remove the seeds and skins. Season with salt and pepper to taste.

» Serve this soup chilled or at room temperature, garnished with Fresh Corn Salsa and a dollop of Chipotle Cream.

Serves 6

Chipotle Cream

» In a bowl, combine the sour cream and chopped chipotle. Taste and add adobo sauce to bring it to the desired level of heat.

Makes 1 cup

Tomato Soup

3 tablespoons extra virgin olive oil

2 pounds ripe tomatoes, cored

6 sprigs fresh cilantro

2 cloves garlic, finely chopped

Salt

Freshly ground black pepper

3 cups Fresh Corn Salsa (page 54)

1 cup Chipotle Cream (recipe follows)

Chipotle Cream

1 cup sour cream (or substitute nonfat plain yogurt)

1 chile from a can of chipotles in adobo sauce, chopped (page 33)

Mango Peach Salsa

Mango Peach Salsa

1 ripe mango, peeled and diced

2 peaches, peeled and diced

Juice of 2 limes

1 red bell pepper, seeded and diced

1 or 2 fresh habaneros, seeded and diced

½ cup fresh cilantro, chopped

1 bunch green onions, thinly sliced, tops included

THIS ONE HAS A BITE TO IT, but the heat of the habanero is offset by the sweetness of the mango and peaches. If you want a less spicy salsa, substitute a jalapeño for the habanero. Handle either kind of chile with care. (page 32)

» Combine the diced mango and peaches, then stir in the lime juice. Add the bell pepper, habaneros, cilantro, and onions. Serve with chips.

» This also makes a nice condiment for fish tacos and grilled shrimp.

Makes 3 cups

Black Bean Salsa

Black Bean Salsa

2 cups cooked black beans, drained (page 62)

½ red bell pepper, stemmed, seeded, and finely diced

½ yellow bell pepper, stemmed, seeded, and finely diced

2 jalapeños, stemmed, seeded, and minced

½ medium yellow onion, finely diced

2 cloves garlic, minced

¼ cup chopped fresh cilantro

2 tablespoons olive oil

Juice of 2 limes

Salt

THIS VERSATILE COMBINATION is equally satisfying as a salad, a side dish, a sauce over grilled meats, or simply as an appetizer with chips.

» In a large bowl, toss the black beans with the red and yellow bell peppers, jalapeños, onion, garlic, cilantro, olive oil, and lime juice. Season to taste with salt.

Makes about 3 cups

MANGO PEACH SALSA

Easy Guacamole

4 large ripe avocados

Juice of 1 lime

1 clove garlic, smashed

1 tablespoon minced onion

Salt

GUACAMOLE IS VERSATILE: salad, salsa, main course, snack. If you want a quick filler for tacos, tostadas, or burritos, this is the guacamole for you. It's also good with grilled meats or fish. If you want to eat it with chips, you can dress it up with peppers, olives, tomatoes, and spices. Once again, do try making your own. It's extremely easy and it's exquisite.

» Peel and pit, then mash the avocados with a fork. Blend in the lime juice, garlic, onion, and salt to taste. Serve immediately.

Makes about 1 cup

VARIATION
Dressed-Up Guacamole

» To the above recipe, add 2 fresh jalapeños, seeded and diced; 2 tomatoes, peeled, seeded and chopped; ¼ cup of chopped fresh cilantro; and one small can of sliced black olives, drained. Mix together and serve immediately with fresh tortilla chips.

DRESSED-UP
GUACAMOLE

BEANS & RICE

MANY TYPES OF BEANS ARE NATIVE TO THE AMERICAS. In fact, until Columbus first noticed local beans under cultivation in the Caribbean, the only bean known to Europeans was the fava or broad bean. The nutrients in these protein-rich seeds form a healthful balance when combined with the nutrients in corn, another native. Served together, they provide all of the nine essential amino acids that humans need to thrive. Rice is a much later arrival, coming from Asia via Spain, but it has been established for centuries in Southwestern, Mexican, and Central and South American cooking. As well as tasting good together, beans and rice, like beans and corn, complement one another nutritionally.

You'll most commonly find dried pinto and black beans in Southwestern cooking, but sometimes pink, white, and kidney beans also turn up. Tepary beans, an indigenous crop grown on tribal lands in Arizona and New Mexico, are making a comeback. Tepary beans are creamy and delicious, but they need a long soak and take several hours to cook, so they do take some planning.

While you can find canned beans in any grocery store, and that's fine for a spur-of-the-moment burrito or tostada, cooking beans from scratch is a more healthful and flavorful way to go. That way you control the salt and other seasonings, and if you make a big batch every month or so, you can freeze them in small quantities and then they're always ready for a quick weeknight dinner.

Rice is another popular ingredient in the Southwest kitchen. If you're on a budget, adding rice to a meat dish, soup, or stew is a thrifty way to stretch the number of servings, and plain rice with a little butter makes a simple and satisfying side dish with meat.

Long grain is a generic classification for rice whose milled grains are at least three times as long as they are wide. Common varieties include basmati, Carolina, jasmine, and Texmati. Long grain rice is the type most commonly used for making Mexican rice, green rice, or similar dishes.

With medium grain rice, the grains are less than three times as long as they are wide, and short grain rice indicates grains that are less than twice as long as they are wide. For puddings, you may prefer the softer texture produced by the shorter grains of rice.

HOW TO COOK RICE AND BEANS

Cooking white rice is easy: Use a heavy saucepan, and the ratio of water to rice should be 2:1. Add about a teaspoon of salt, bring to a boil, then cover and turn the heat down to a very low simmer. Cook for about 20 minutes or until all of the water is gone, then remove from heat and let the rice sit covered for another five minutes. Fluff it up with a fork and you're ready to eat. Brown rice takes longer (about 45 minutes), but the process is the same. Be sure you wash the rice well before cooking to eliminate any excess starch and to remove any chemical residues that might remain from the cultivation process.

There are several different and equally successful ways to cook beans, depending on the cook's time, equipment, and temperament. And beans themselves vary in the cooking they require, according to their size, variety, and freshness (the fresher, the quicker).

The first step is to buy them in bulk in a grocery where there's lots of turnover. Old beans sometimes never soften and have little flavor. All beans should be carefully picked over before cooking. A good way to do this is to pour them out onto a baking pan, methodically inspect them, and remove any small stones, dirt clods, broken or misshapen beans, or other detritus, and then wash them well.

To cook beans faster, soak them first. One way is to allow them to soak overnight in a cool place: Just put them in a large bowl and cover with plenty of water. If you notice the beans are absorbing all the water, add more to cover. Or quick-soak them by covering them with water, bringing them to a boil for 2 minutes, and then letting them stand covered for an hour. Either soaking treatment will shorten cooking time by a third or half.

Soaked or not, any type of beans can simply be simmered on the stovetop until tender. First drain away the soaking water, if any, and put the beans in a large stockpot. Add water to cover by at least 2 inches and bring to a boil. Reduce the heat, cover, and let simmer for anywhere from one to three hours, depending on the type of bean. Add salt in the last hour of cooking.

In a pressure cooker at full pressure, unsoaked beans will usually cook in about an hour, while soaked beans will be ready in about 40 minutes. Release the pressure then add salt and simmer a few more minutes to finish. In a slow cooker, presoaked beans require 3–4 hours on high, or 5–6 hours on low; unsoaked beans take proportionally longer. But again, this varies according to freshness and type of bean, so watch and taste to be sure.

As the beans near completion, taste to make sure they are tender, and no matter how you cook them, be sure to use ample water, as beans scorch easily. When in doubt, add more water since you can always drain it or boil it off later. When the beans are done, you can freeze them in 2 to 4 cup portions for later use. They should not sit long at room temperature or be stored in the refrigerator for more than 3 days.

Cowboy Pinto Beans

ALWAYS A FAVORITE at Western barbecues.

» Wash and soak the beans. Drain, then place in a 2-quart saucepan and cover with 2 inches of water. Add the salt pork, onion, bell pepper, garlic, jalapeño, cumin, epazote, tomato sauce, and coffee. Bring to a boil.

Reduce heat and simmer for at least 2 hours, or until beans are very tender. Add salt to taste, but only after the beans are completely soft.

Serves 4

VARIATION

Borracho (Drunk) Beans

» Replace the coffee with a 12-ounce bottle of Mexican beer such as Negra Modelo or Dos Equis Amber.

2 cups dry pinto beans, picked over and soaked overnight in cold water to cover

½ pound salt pork or 4 slices thick-cut bacon, chopped

½ cup chopped onion

½ cup chopped bell pepper (red or green)

2 cloves garlic, smashed

1 jalapeño, chopped

2 teaspoons ground cumin

3 sprigs epazote

1 can (8 ounces) tomato sauce or petite diced tomatoes

1 cup brewed coffee

Salt

Refritos *(Refried Beans)*

Refritos

2 pounds dry pinto beans

1 tablespoon salt

6 tablespoons lard

1 cup grated cheddar or crumbled queso fresco, for garnish

A STAPLE IN MEXICAN CUISINE, refritos can be used as a side dish, wrapped in a flour tortilla to make a burrito, used as taco filling, or even to fill tamales. Don't replace the lard with another form of oil—the beans just won't taste the same. It's better to eat them plain.

» Wash and soak the beans. Drain and then place the beans in a large stockpot and cover with cold water. Bring to a boil over high heat, then reduce heat to low and cover. Simmer for 1½ hours. Add salt and simmer for another hour or until beans are very soft. Remove from heat and strain, reserving the cooking liquid.

» Return the beans to the pot and mash with a potato masher or the back of a large spoon. In a small skillet, heat 4 tablespoons of lard until it's very hot but not smoking. Pour into the mashed beans and stir well. Add the cooking liquid and simmer over low heat until the beans are thick, stirring frequently. Heat the remaining two tablespoons of lard until hot and add to beans. Stir well. Remove from heat and garnish with cheese.

Serves 12

Spanish Black Beans

Spanish Black Beans

¼ cup olive oil

½ cup chopped onion

½ cup chopped green bell pepper

½ cup chopped red bell pepper

3 garlic cloves, finely chopped

2 teaspoons ground cumin

2 tablespoons tomato paste

4 cups cooked black beans

1 cup chicken stock

¼ cup chopped green onions

¼ cup chopped fresh cilantro

THE FLAVOR OF THESE BLACK BEANS continues to improve after a day, so you may want to make them ahead and reheat just before serving.

» In a heavy-bottomed saucepan, heat the olive oil and then sauté the onions and the green and red bell peppers until softened. Add the garlic, cumin, and tomato paste, and stir to combine. Add the black beans and broth, bring to a boil, and then reduce the heat and simmer 20 minutes.

» Stir in the green onions and cilantro.

Serves 4–6

Black Bean Soup

DEMURE IN APPEARANCE, but lively in the mouth!

» Wash and sort the beans and soak overnight.

» Drain and rinse the beans and place in a stockpot. Cover with water and bring to a boil. Add bay leaf, onion, garlic, and jalapeños. Cover, reduce heat, and cook until tender, approximately 1½ hours.

» When the beans are tender, remove from heat and stir in salt, pepper, and chicken or vegetable stock. Use an immersion blender to puree the mixture, or add in batches to a food processor or blender. If the soup is too thick, add more stock to thin. Reheat to serving temperature. Ladle into bowls and garnish with a dollop of sour cream and a sprinkle of cilantro.

Serves 6

1 pound dry black beans

1 bay leaf

1 large onion, minced

3 cloves garlic, chopped

2 jalapeños, seeded and chopped

1 teaspoon salt

½ teaspoon freshly ground black pepper

1 cup chicken or vegetable stock

Sour cream, for garnish

Fresh cilantro, chopped, for garnish

Sopa de Frijoles

1 pound dried kidney beans

8 cups vegetable stock

1 large onion, minced

2 cloves garlic, minced

1 teaspoon dried Mexican orégano

2 teaspoons salt

3 tablespoons extra virgin olive oil

½ cup tomato sauce

2 tablespoons red wine vinegar

6 mint leaves, finely chopped

Croutons, for garnish

THIS SOUP GETS A FINAL FLAVOR spark from a sprinkle of mint and vinegar.

» Wash and soak the beans. Drain and discard the soaking water and add the beans to a large stockpot. Cover with the vegetable stock and add the onion, garlic, and oregano. Bring to a boil over high heat, then reduce heat to low, cover, and simmer for 1 to 1½ hours or until the beans are soft. Add the salt in the last half-hour of cooking.

» Cool slightly, then drain the beans, reserving the liquid. Return the beans to the pot and mash slightly with a potato masher or the back of a spoon. Heat the olive oil until very hot and pour into the beans, stirring well. Slowly stir in the reserved liquid and the tomato sauce and heat over medium heat for about 15 minutes until heated through and well blended. Adjust seasonings to taste.

» Combine the vinegar and mint leaves in a small cruet. Serve the soup in bowls garnished with croutons, and pass the minted vinegar to sprinkle on the top of the soup.

Serves 6

White Bean Chicken Chili

THIS IS A SIMPLE WAY to use leftover chicken, and because it cooks so quickly, it's an easy midweek supper, especially good with a side of corn bread or warm tortillas. To peel tomatoes, dip them into boiling water for a minute or two to loosen the peel, and then it should slip off easily.

» Heat the oil in a large stockpot. Add the onion and garlic and sauté until the onion is translucent, about 5 minutes. Add the tomatillos, tomatoes, green chile, and chicken stock. Add the oregano and cumin. Bring to a boil, then reduce heat and cook for 5 minutes

» Add the corn, chicken, and white beans. Cover and simmer for another 15 minutes. Add salt and pepper, adjusting the seasonings as necessary.

» Serve with a squeeze of lime and a dollop of sour cream.

Serves 6

2 tablespoons oil

1 medium onion, diced

2 cloves garlic, diced

1 pound tomatillos, shucked, roasted, and chopped

2 large tomatoes, peeled, seeded, and chopped

4 green chiles, roasted, peeled, seeded, and chopped (page 32)

1 quart chicken stock

1 teaspoon dried Mexican oregano

1 teaspoon ground cumin

1 cup fresh or frozen corn kernels

1 pound cooked chicken, diced or shredded

2 cups cooked white beans

1 teaspoon salt

½ teaspoon freshly ground black pepper

2 limes, cut into wedges, for garnish

Sour cream, for garnish

Navajo Tacos with Fry Bread

Navajo Tacos

Fry Bread (recipe follows)

1 quart Cowboy Pinto Beans (page 63)

1 small head lettuce, shredded

2 tomatoes, chopped

1 onion, chopped

½ pound longhorn cheese, grated

Fresh salsa (page 52)

Fry Bread

2 cups flour

½ teaspoon salt

2½ teaspoons baking powder

2 tablespoons shortening

¾ cup warm water

Oil for frying

HERE'S THE HOMEMADE VERSION of a mouthwatering Native American specialty, often found at fairs, fiestas, and roadside stands.

» Heat the oven to 200 degrees F.

» Prepare each plate by placing one piece of fry bread on an oven-safe dish and topping it with ½ cup of beans. Keep the dishes warm in the oven as you prepare each one. When they're ready to be served, add the lettuce, tomatoes, onions, and grated cheese. Serve the salsa in a bowl so that it can be added at each person's discretion.

Serves 6

Fry Bread

Hot and fresh from the frying pan, this is a very special treat.

» Combine the flour, salt, and baking powder and mix in the shortening with your fingers. Blend in the water with a fork. Knead the dough until smooth. Divide the dough into 6 equal balls and roll each ball into an 8-inch circle approximately ½ inch thick, about twice the thickness of a tortilla. Fry the circles in hot oil until golden brown, turning so both sides are evenly cooked, and drain on paper towels.

Serves 6

Green Rice

Green Rice

½ onion, diced

2 tablespoons olive oil

2 cloves garlic, finely chopped

1½ cups long-grain white rice

3 cups chicken or vegetable stock

½ cup finely chopped fresh cilantro

½ cup finely chopped fresh parsley

Salt

THIS BRIGHTLY COLORED RICE is very pretty. Use it for its flavor, but also to liven up a meal that would otherwise be visually boring.

» In a saucepan over medium heat, sauté the onion in the olive oil until softened. Add the garlic and sauté 1 more minute. Add the rice and stir until the rice is coated with oil and heated through. Add the chicken stock and bring to a boil.

» Cover the pan, reduce heat to low, and cook for 20 minutes, or until tender. Remove from heat, stir in the cilantro and parsley, and add salt to taste.

Serves 4

Spanish Rice

Spanish Rice

1 tablespoon olive oil

1½ cups uncooked long-grain white rice

1 small white onion, chopped fine

2 medium cloves garlic, minced

1 can (8 ounces) tomato sauce

3 cups water

2 cups diced tomatoes

1 teaspoon salt

1 teaspoon ground cumin

1 big pinch saffron

A TRADITIONAL RECIPE FROM OLD NEW MEXICO, cooked uncovered in Spanish fashion.

» Heat the oil in a large frying pan on medium heat. Brown the rice, stirring constantly, for about 3 or 4 minutes. Add the onion and garlic and sauté with the rice; then add the tomato sauce and water and bring to a boil. Quickly lower the heat to a simmer, add the fresh tomatoes, salt, and cumin, and cook for 20 minutes, stirring occasionally. Remove it from the heat, sprinkle the saffron on top, and let it stand (covered) for 15 minutes before serving.

Serves 8

Albóndigas

ALBÓNDIGAS ARE MEATBALLS, another traditional favorite on the border. It's also fun just to say the word: "all-BONE-dee-gahs!"

» In a large bowl, combine the ground beef, ground pork, salt, pepper, garlic, eggs, and masa harina. Use your hands to mix well. Add half of the cilantro, onion, and tomatoes to the meat mixture and mix well, again using your hands. Roll the mixture into balls about 1 inch in diameter.

» Bring the water to a boil. Add the remaining half of the cilantro, onions, and tomatoes, and then add the rice and mint leaves. Add the meatballs, reduce heat to low, cover, and simmer until the rice and meat are cooked, about 45 minutes. Ladle into bowls, garnish with lime and cilantro, and serve.

Serves 8

1½ pounds lean ground beef

½ pound ground pork

1 teaspoon salt

1 teaspoon freshly ground black pepper

2 cloves garlic, minced

2 eggs

4 tablespoons masa harina (page 8)

1 bunch fresh cilantro, minced

1 medium onion, finely diced

5 medium tomatoes, finely chopped

3 quarts water

1 cup uncooked rice

3 fresh mint leaves, chopped

Lime wedges and fresh cilantro, for garnish

MEATS, POULTRY & FISH

IN THE SOUTHWEST, MAIN COURSES MAY BE COOKED ON A STOVETOP, in an oven, or over a fire. Fish and poultry are popular as well as various red meats, and all these techniques and ingredients are represented here—with a special emphasis on outdoor cooking.

Even though we all live inside and have modern kitchens with every conceivable convenience, there's still something primal about cooking over an open flame, listening to the sizzle of the meat, and breathing in the aroma of wood smoke. Grilling is a big part of Southwestern cooking because it imparts a special flavor you can't get any other way. And there's also the fact that cooking outdoors is more convivial than crowding all of your guests into a cramped kitchen. Barbecuing, which is slow-roasting meat over a low fire, inspires fanaticism and good-natured rivalry all over the country. Grilling, on the other hand, involves a quick sear on a hot flame.

Some people prefer their grilled meats with a little sprinkle of salt and pepper and nothing else, but if you want to add a Southwestern flavor, the easiest way is to make your own rubs, marinades, and barbecue sauces.

Marinating is a good technique to add flavor and tenderize beef, pork, or poultry. It requires advance planning because the meat has to sit in the sauce for several hours or overnight.

Rubs are combinations of spices and herbs that go on the meat shortly before it goes on the heat. It's fun to experiment with different combinations on different cuts and types of meat.

Barbecue sauce usually goes on the meat right after it comes off the fire. While you can buy bottled sauce and probably be happy, it's another one of those things that's easy to make and gives you a better result.

The nice thing about using rubs, marinades, and sauces is that you can add extra flavor to vegetables and inexpensive cuts of meat, impressing your family and friends with your culinary genius.

Spiced Citrus Marinade

Spiced Citrus Marinade

2 tablespoons cumin seeds

4 large garlic cloves

1 tablespoon salt

1 tablespoon dried oregano

2 dried serrano chiles, crumbled into flakes

¼ cup achiote paste

½ cup fresh orange juice

½ cup fresh lime juice

ACHIOTE IS MADE FROM GROUND ANNATTO seeds and can be found in Mexican groceries or spice suppliers. This marinade is excellent on pork roast or chicken.

» In a small skillet over medium heat, toast the cumin seeds, stirring frequently until fragrant and lightly browned. Set aside to cool.

» Finely mince the garlic into a paste, and then, using your hands, knead in the salt. Place the garlic paste into a bowl and add the toasted cumin, oregano, chiles, achiote paste, orange juice, and lime juice. Whisk together and pour over the meat.

Makes enough for one pork roast or chicken (3–5 pounds)

Coffee Fajita Marinade

Coffee Fajita Marinade

¼ cup apple cider vinegar

2 tablespoons brewed coffee

2 tablespoons Worcestershire sauce

2 tablespoons liquid smoke

2 tablespoons soy sauce

1 tablespoon brown sugar

3 cloves garlic, smashed

½ teaspoon dried oregano

½ teaspoon freshly ground black pepper

½ teaspoon salt

½ teaspoon lemon pepper seasoning

¼ teaspoon ground cumin

THIS MAKES A GREAT MARINADE for chicken or skirt steak.

» Combine all ingredients in a large plastic zipper bag. Add up to 2 pounds of chicken or skirt steak, cut into strips. Seal the bag and let the meat marinate for at least 1 hour and as long as 24 hours before grilling or sautéing.

Makes enough for 2 pounds of meat

HOW TO GRILL THE PERFECT STEAK

Grilling a steak is about the easiest thing to do, but the key to a really great steak is to treat the meat kindly at every step of the process.

First, defrost the steaks in the refrigerator for a couple of days if they're frozen. Never defrost meat at room temperature.

After they're defrosted, let the steaks come to room temperature. Cover them and let them sit on the counter for 30 minutes to an hour, depending on thickness. You can do this while the grill is heating up.

When it's time to cook, pat the steaks dry with a paper towel. Trim away any excess fat. Melt a teaspoon of butter per steak and brush each steak on both sides with the butter. Coat with the rub of your choice. Be generous. If you're in a minimalist mood, just use salt and freshly ground black pepper.

Place the steaks on the hottest part of the grill. Let them cook for three minutes, then use a pair of tongs to turn and cook for three minutes more. The total amount of time on the grill will depend on the thickness of the steak. A 1½-inch-thick steak will take about 12 minutes to get to rare, so flip it two more times. You don't want to flip more than three times, and never pierce the steak with a fork. Use tongs.

Knowing when the steak is done to your liking is the tricky part. An instant read thermometer is the most accurate. A rare steak should be between 110 and 115 degrees F, medium rare is about 120, medium is 125–130, and well done is 140. If you want to impress your friends, you can use the finger test. Poke the steak in the middle with your finger. If it feels like the flesh on your palm at the base of your thumb, it's rare. If it feels like the middle of your palm, then it's well done. It may take some practice, but you'll get the hang of it.

After the steaks come off the grill, cover them and allow them to sit for 5 minutes. This lets the juices redistribute through the meat. If you want a steakhouse flavor, put a pat of butter on each steak while it's resting.

That's all there is to it. Now pour a nice glass of Cabernet and enjoy!

Espresso-Chile Steak Rub

Espresso-Chile Steak Rub

4 teaspoons espresso powder

1 teaspoon garlic powder

1½ teaspoons freshly ground black pepper

1 teaspoon salt

1 teaspoon smoked paprika

1 teaspoon dried oregano

½ teaspoon dried thyme

¼ teaspoon ground dried chipotle chile

Cocoa-Coffee Spice Rub

6 tablespoons paprika

2 tablespoons salt

2 tablespoons cocoa powder

2 tablespoons espresso powder

2 tablespoons garlic powder

2 tablespoons brown sugar

1 tablespoon freshly ground black pepper

THE DARK COLOR OF THE RUB gives a "blackened" effect—a nice contrast to the pink of a steak cooked to a perfect medium or medium-rare.

» Mix together all ingredients in a small bowl. Thickly coat steaks with the mixture before grilling or broiling.

Makes about ¼ cup (enough for 2 large steaks)

Cocoa-Coffee Spice Rub

NATIVE AMERICANS USED CHOCOLATE as a savory drink long before the advent of candy, so the use of cocoa as a spice makes perfect sense. This is especially good on pork roast or steak. This recipe makes a plentiful amount, so store any extra in a tightly sealed container for up to six months.

» Mix together all ingredients in a small bowl. Thickly coat pork roast or steak before grilling or roasting.

Makes about 1 cup

Coffee Barbecue Sauce

THIS IS ESPECIALLY GOOD on tender baby back ribs, but also try it on grilled steaks or other meats.

» Combine the ketchup, coffee, orange juice, honey, liquid smoke, soy sauce, pepper, salt, and Tabasco in a small bowl and mix well. Use as a basting sauce for grilled meats in the last 5 minutes of cooking time, to prevent flare-ups and burned meat.

Makes about 1 cup

Jalapeño-Lime Barbecue Sauce

SERVE WITH COUNTRY-STYLE SPARERIBS, burgers, or anything else from the grill. Control the heat by adding to or reducing the number of jalapeños.

» Mix ketchup, vinegar, jalapeños, molasses, lime juice, vegetable juice, and garlic in a small saucepan. Heat over medium and then lower the heat so that the sauce barely simmers for 20 minutes or until thickened.

Makes 1½ cups

Coffee Barbecue Sauce

½ cup ketchup

¼ cup brewed coffee

2 tablespoons orange juice concentrate

1 tablespoon honey

1½ teaspoons liquid smoke

1 teaspoon soy sauce

1 teaspoon freshly ground black pepper

½ teaspoon salt

¼–½ teaspoon chipotle-flavored Tabasco sauce

Jalapeño Lime Barbecue Sauce

½ cup ketchup

¼ cup balsamic vinegar

2–4 jalapeños, seeded and finely minced

¼ cup dark molasses

Juice of 1 lime

1 can (5½ ounces) vegetable juice, such as V-8

2 cloves garlic, smashed

Lamb Stew

½ cup flour, plus 2 tablespoons

½ teaspoon salt

½ teaspoon freshly ground black pepper

2 pounds boneless lamb, cubed

2 tablespoons vegetable oil

2 quarts water, plus 1 cup

1 large onion, chopped

3 celery ribs, diced

4 carrots, cut into 1-inch chunks

6 russet potatoes, peeled and cut into ½-inch chunks

1 can (14½-ounce) stewed tomatoes

3 yellow squash or zucchinis, sliced

Fry bread (page 68)

LAMB STEW IS A STAPLE in Native American cultures, and it makes a hearty dinner, especially when served with traditional fry bread.

» Combine ½ cup flour, salt, and pepper in a plastic zipper bag. Add meat in small batches and shake until each piece is completely covered.

» Heat the oil in a stockpot and brown the meat over medium-high heat in small batches. When all of the meat is browned, add it back into the pot.

» Use a little water to deglaze the pan, and then add 2 quarts water and bring to a boil. Reduce heat, cover, and simmer for 30 minutes. Add the onion, celery, carrots, and potatoes. Cover and continue to simmer another 30 minutes or until the vegetables are tender. Add tomatoes and squash.

» Whisk the 2 tablespoons of flour into the 1 cup of water until the flour is completely dissolved. Stir into the stew. Season to taste with salt and pepper. Cover and simmer another 10 minutes or until the squash is cooked and the stew has thickened.

» Ladle over fry bread to serve.

Serves 8

Chile-Braised Lamb Shanks with Cilantro Gremolata

1 pound dried red chiles (New Mexico or pasilla)

4 cloves garlic, finely chopped

2 teaspoons ground cumin

Juice of 1 lemon

½ teaspoon salt

4 lamb shanks

2 cups dark beer such as Negra Modelo

Cilantro Gremolata (recipe follows)

THIS IS BASED ON A RECIPE developed by the American Lamb Board, and we've enhanced it with gremolata (a pungent cilantro and lemon garnish). It is normally made with parsley and served with osso buco, the Italian dish of braised veal shanks. Because lamb shanks are so much smaller than veal shanks, use one whole shank per person. Serve with polenta or mashed potatoes.

» Preheat the oven to 350 degrees F.

» Arrange the chiles on a baking sheet and toast 2–5 minutes, until they smell toasted but before they burn. Remove them from the oven and set aside.

» When the chiles are cool enough to handle, remove the stems and seeds. Tear the chiles into pieces and put them into a large saucepan. Add enough water to cover, bring to a boil, then turn off the heat and allow the chiles to soak until completely softened.

» Drain and reserve most of the water. Transfer the chiles to a blender and puree, adding just enough of the reserved water to make a thick, smooth paste. Strain the mixture through a fine sieve. Add the garlic, cumin, lemon juice, and salt.

» Trim any excess fat from the lamb shanks. Cover the meat with the chile paste and let it marinate in the refrigerator overnight.

» Preheat the oven to 325 degrees F.

» Place the meat in a deep roasting pan. Add the beer and enough water to come halfway up the sides of the shanks. Cover the pan with foil and cook until the meat is very tender.

» Remove the shanks from the pan. Skim the fat from the pan drippings and whisk in enough water to make a rich sauce.

» Serve the lamb with plenty of sauce, garnished with Cilantro Gremolata (recipe follows).

Serves 4

Cilantro Gremolata

» Combine all ingredients in a small bowl.

Makes ¼ cup

Grilled Flank or Skirt Steak with Mole Verde

FLANK STEAK IS A FLAVORFUL cut that comes, literally, from the belly of the beast. Skirt steak is also full of flavor, but don't overcook either of them, or they will toughen. If you have leftover slices of steak, reheat them in a pan, toss with any mole, and tuck into a toasted bun for a quick and tasty sandwich.

» Using a mortar and pestle, crush the garlic and salt into a paste. In a small bowl, combine the garlic paste, cumin, oregano, black pepper, and olive oil.

» Lay the flank steak on a cutting board and make a series of shallow, crisscrossed cuts on the surface of the meat; flip and repeat on the other side. This will help the marinade penetrate and keep the meat from curling on the grill.

» Rub the meat all over with the garlic and herb mixture and put it in a resealable plastic container or large zippered storage bag. Allow the meat to rest in the refrigerator 2 hours or overnight.

» Preheat the grill to high. Leave the meat in the refrigerator until just before you put it on the grill. Grill to medium rare, about 4-5 minutes on each side. Transfer the steak to a platter, cover with foil, and allow it to rest 10 minutes.

» Meanwhile, in a small saucepan, heat the Mole Verde.

» Slice the flank steak against the grain into thin strips. Serve drizzled with mole.

Serves 4

Cilantro Gremolata

3 tablespoons finely chopped cilantro leaves

3 cloves garlic, finely chopped

Finely grated zest of 1 large lemon

Grilled Flank or Skirt Steak with Mole Verde

6 cloves garlic, minced

1 teaspoon salt

2 tablespoons ground cumin

1 tablespoon dried Mexican oregano

1 teaspoon freshly ground black pepper

1 tablespoon olive oil

1½ pounds flank or skirt steak

2 cups Mole Verde (page 50)

Flank Steak with Creamy Rajas

1 pound fresh poblano chiles, roasted, peeled, and seeded

1 large onion, peeled

1 tablespoon butter

½ cup heavy cream

1 flank steak (1½ pounds), trimmed of excess fat

½ teaspoon ground cumin

½ teaspoon ground coriander

Salt

Freshly ground black pepper

8 flour tortillas

THE SLICED PEPPERS THAT ACCOMPANY this steak are called rajas in Spanish. You can use either poblanos or New Mexico green chiles for this recipe, and the simple, delicious sauce also complements other lean grilled meats and poultry. Save a few chile slices for a colorful garnish.

» Slice the chiles into ½-inch-wide strips. Set them aside.

» Slice the onion in half from the stem to the root end. Slice into ½-inch-wide strips.

» In a heavy skillet, melt the butter and sauté the onions until they are softened and starting to brown. Add the chiles. Add the cream and simmer for 5 minutes, or until the mixture thickens.

» Sprinkle the steak with cumin, coriander, salt, and pepper. Grill or broil for 5–8 minutes on each side, or until it reaches the desired level of doneness (page 75). Remove from the heat and allow to rest 10 minutes.

» Holding your knife at a 45-degree angle, slice the steak into thin strips. Serve with warm tortillas and creamy rajas.

Serves 4

Chorizo

Chorizo

3½ pounds ground beef

1¼ cups chile powder

6 cloves garlic, finely minced

½ teaspoon dried cilantro

¾ teaspoon dried Mexican oregano

2 tablespoons apple cider vinegar

2 cups canned tomato sauce

2 teaspoons salt

1 teaspoon freshly ground black pepper

Chorizo and Egg Breakfast Scramble

1 pound chorizo

6 eggs

3 large potatoes, peeled and grated

Salt

Freshly ground black pepper

6 large flour tortillas, warmed

1 cup grated asadero or Monterey Jack cheese

IN SPAIN, CHORIZO IS A HARD, CURED SAUSAGE, but in the Southwest, chorizo is a fresh mix of meat, chile powder, and seasonings. This recipe calls for ground beef, but you can also use pork or a combination. Be sure to use high-quality ground meat with a 90:10 or 85:15 fat ratio and pure chile powder, and your chorizo will be healthful as well as tasty.

» In a large bowl, place the ground beef, chile powder, garlic, cilantro, oregano, vinegar, tomato sauce, salt, and pepper. Mix with your hands until the ingredients are incorporated, but don't overmix.

» Form into a large loaf and wrap tightly in plastic. Refrigerate for 2 to 3 days to allow the flavors to mellow. At that point, the chorizo may be cooked or frozen.

Makes 3.5 pounds

Chorizo and Egg Breakfast Scramble

IF YOU USE STORE-BOUGHT CHORIZO, try to choose the highest quality and be sure to drain any excess fat on paper towels before serving. For a quick breakfast to go, turn it into a burrito.

» In a large skillet, cook the chorizo over medium heat, stirring with a wooden spoon to break up any chunks. Drain any excess grease, if necessary. When the meat is cooked through but not browned, crack the eggs into the skillet and stir into the chorizo. When the eggs are set, remove the mixture to a warm bowl and cover. Set aside.

» While the chorizo is cooking, drain the grated potatoes in a colander lined with paper towels. When drained, pat dry.

» To the same skillet add the grated potatoes. Sprinkle with salt and pepper and cook, turning, until browned on both sides.

» For burritos, place a generous helping of the chorizo, potatoes, and cheese on each tortilla and serve with your favorite salsa.

Serves 6

CHORIZO AND EGG
BREAKFAST SCRAMBLE

Green Chile Cheeseburger

2 pounds ground beef

2 eggs

1 teaspoon salt

1 teaspoon freshly ground black pepper

Olive oil

4 green chiles, roasted seeded, and peeled

8 slices cheddar cheese

8 large hamburger buns

Mustard, mayonnaise, ketchup

Lettuce, sliced onions, sliced tomatoes, sliced dill pickles

THE GOOD OLD ALL-AMERICAN BURGER is a staple during the summer grilling season. While you can keep it basic, you can also add some distinctive regional touches. Some tips for creating a great burger: Use good ground beef with an 85:15 lean-to-fat ratio. Handle the meat gently when you're mixing it. And never smash the burgers on the grill; use a spatula to flip them.

» Heat the grill to medium high.

» In a large bowl, mix the ground beef, eggs, salt, and pepper, using your hands and taking care to incorporate the ingredients just until well-blended but not overmixed.

» Roll the meat into 8 equal-size balls. Pat into rounds with your hands. Brush each burger on both sides with olive oil.

» Place the burgers on the grill and cook for three minutes. Turn and cook to desired doneness.

» In the last few minutes on the grill, top the burger with roasted, seeded, and peeled green chile strips, followed by a piece of cheddar cheese. Allow the cheese to melt before removing the burger from the heat.

» Remove from the grill and tent with foil to keep warm. Place the buns on the grill, sliced side down, and brown lightly.

» To serve, place the buns in a basket and arrange the condiments, allowing each guest to build their favorite burger.

Makes 8 burgers

VARIATION *Spicy Chipotle Burger*

» Add two minced chipotles in adobo and a tablespoon of adobo sauce (page 33) to the meat mixture. Top with a tablespoon of Garlic Chipotle Barbecue Sauce (page 92).

Bison Burgers with Pepita Pesto

BISON MEAT IS VERY LEAN, and it benefits from the rich flavor of this shelled pumpkin seed (pepita) pesto. You can use any leftover pesto on black beans or nachos, or tossed with pasta.

» Heat the grill to high.

» In a large bowl, combine the meat and pesto. Form the mixture into 4 patties. Grill over medium heat until the burgers reach the desired level of doneness.

» Brush the rolls with the olive oil and toast them on the grill until golden.

» Serve the burgers garnished with lettuce, tomato, avocado, and onion.

Makes 4 burgers

Pepita Pesto

» In a heavy skillet over medium-high heat, toast the pumpkin seeds until most of them are puffed. Remove them from the heat and allow to cool.

» In a blender or food processor, process the cilantro, garlic, toasted pumpkin seeds, and Parmesan. With the machine running, add the olive oil

in a thin stream. Season to taste with salt and pepper.

» Use immediately or store in the refrigerator for up to a week.

Makes about 2 cups

Bison Burgers with Pepita Pesto

1 pound ground bison

¼ cup Pepita Pesto (recipe follows)

4 hearty rolls, split

3 tablespoons olive oil

Lettuce, tomato, avocado, and onion, for garnish

Pepita Pesto

½ cup pepitas

2 cups coarsely chopped fresh cilantro leaves

3 cloves garlic, finely chopped

¼ cup grated Parmesan cheese

¼ cup extra virgin olive oil

Salt

Freshly ground black pepper

Turkey Mole Burgers

½ cup mole (pages 49, 50)

1½ pounds ground turkey

1 teaspoon chile powder

4 flour tortillas or rolls

¼ cup mayonnaise

Iceberg lettuce leaves

Tomato slices

USE YOUR OWN MOLE (pages 49, 50) or substitute store-bought sauce; either delivers a quick dose of flavor to turkey, which can be dry and bland. Look for jars of mole in the Mexican foods section of your supermarket, where popular brands include Doña Maria, Rogelio Bueno, and El Mexicano. You can wrap these burgers up in warm, fluffy, freshly made flour tortillas, or you can also use crusty Mexican bolillo rolls or other buns.

» Heat the grill to high.

» In a large bowl, combine the mole, turkey, and chile powder. Gently form into 4 patties.

» Grill the burgers over high heat until they reach your desired level of doneness. Remove the burgers and warm the tortillas or rolls briefly on the grill.

» Spread about 1 tablespoon of mayonnaise on the center of each tortilla or bun. Top with iceberg lettuce, tomato slices, and a hot burger. If you are using tortillas, fold the tortilla up around the burger. Serve immediately.

Serves 4

Grilled Orange Turkey

HUNDREDS OF YEARS BEFORE THE FIRST THANKSGIVING, Southwesterners were eating turkey. If you're lucky enough to live in a warm climate at Thanksgiving, grilling the turkey is a nice alternative to oven roasting. If it's too cold to fire up the grill, you can also do this in the oven; just follow the roasting directions that come with the turkey.

» Using indirect heat method (with the lid closed and the meat positioned away from the fire), place a foil drip pan in the grill and preheat to medium.

» Remove the giblets from the turkey and set aside for another use. Rinse and pat dry the turkey. Work the softened butter underneath the turkey skin, then place the orange, apple, and onion pieces in the body cavity. Sprinkle with salt, tuck the wing ends under, and secure the legs.

» Insert a meat thermometer into the breast or thigh, taking care not to touch bone, and making sure that it won't interfere with the grill cover. Place the turkey on the grill over the drip pan and cover the grill. Baste periodically with a mixture of the orange juice and white wine, and roast until the thermometer reads 170 degrees F, approximately 3-4 hours. Remove from the grill and allow to rest for about 30 minutes before carving.

Serves 6

1 fresh turkey (12–14 pounds)

1 stick of butter, softened

1 orange, cut into eighths, peel on

1 apple, cored and sliced

1 onion, quartered

Salt

2 cups fresh orange juice

1 cup white wine

Chicken Wings in Mole

4 pounds chicken wings

Salt

Freshly ground black pepper

4 cups mole

¼ cup toasted sesame seeds

THESE ZINGY WINGS ARE PERFECT PARTY FOOD because they're easy to make ahead of time and people love them. They taste best with either homemade Mole Poblano or Mole Verde.

» Arrange the chicken wings in 2 shallow baking pans. Sprinkle liberally with salt and pepper. Broil for 10–15 minutes, turning once, until the wings are golden and crispy.

» Transfer the wings to a large, deep saucepan and pour the mole over them. Add water as necessary to thin the mole enough to cover the wings. Bring to a boil, reduce heat, and simmer 30 minutes. Sprinkle with toasted sesame seeds and serve.

Serves 6

Taquitos with Chicken or Beef

SOME PEOPLE CALL THESE FLAUTAS, which means flutes. They are supposed to be quite crisp and are a bit of a trick to handle, so don't be dismayed if it takes a while to learn the technique. They're a good party snack but can make a meal as well, served with beans and rice.

» Fry the corn tortillas in hot oil for a few seconds, just to soften them, and then drain them on paper towels. Spoon approximately 2 tablespoons of chicken or ground beef and 1 teaspoon of onion onto each tortilla. Roll the filled tortillas into "flutes" and secure with toothpicks. Sauté in batches in a skillet, or use a pair of tongs to hold each flute in heated deeper oil just long enough to cook it to a crisp. Drain them on paper towels, remove toothpicks, and top with shredded lettuce and chopped tomato. Serve guacamole and sour cream on the side.

Makes 1 dozen

Taquitos with Chicken or Beef

1 dozen corn tortillas

1 pound cooked and shredded chicken or browned lean ground beef

½ medium onion, finely chopped

Vegetable oil

Shredded lettuce

Chopped tomatoes

Guacamole and sour cream for garnish (optional)

Pecan Chile Chicken

BECAUSE THE SAUCE IS RICH, this dish works well with rice and steamed asparagus on the side.

» With a mallet, gently pound the chicken breasts to a consistent thickness and set aside.

» Combine the ground pecans, chile powder, cocoa powder, garlic powder, cumin, pepper, and ½ teaspoon salt in a plastic zipper bag and shake until well blended. Add the chicken breasts one at a time and shake until coated.

» Heat the olive oil in a deep skillet until hot, then add the prepared chicken breasts. Sauté about 2-3 minutes, then turn and sauté about another minute or two. It's important to not overcook. Remove the chicken to a serving platter, and tent with foil to keep warm.

» Add butter to the skillet and scrape the bottom of the pan while it melts. Add the half-and-half, ½ teaspoon salt, and chopped pecans, then heat until slightly reduced and thick. Pour this sauce over the chicken to serve.

Serves 6

Pecan Chile Chicken

6 boneless, skinless chicken breasts

½ cup finely ground pecans

2 tablespoons chile powder

2 tablespoons cocoa powder

1 tablespoon garlic powder

1 teaspoon ground cumin

1 teaspoon freshly ground black pepper

1 teaspoon salt, divided

2 teaspoons olive oil

2 tablespoons butter

½ cup half-and-half

½ cup chopped pecans

Grilled Chicken with Garlic-Chipotle Barbecue Sauce

¾ cup ketchup

½ cup water

¼ cup apple cider vinegar

5 garlic cloves, smashed

½ yellow or white onion, chopped

Juice of 1 lime

3 tablespoons dark brown sugar

1 tablespoon Worcestershire sauce

1 teaspoon chipotle-flavored
  Tabasco sauce

1 teaspoon freshly ground black
  pepper

4 large skin-on chicken breasts

Kosher or sea salt

THE BARBECUE SAUCE CAN BE MADE several days ahead and stored in the refrigerator until you're ready to grill. Make sure to brush it on only during the last 5 minutes or so of grilling so it doesn't cause flare-ups and burn the chicken. Customize the sauce by replacing the water with fruit juice or wine.

» In a medium saucepan, mix together the ketchup, water, vinegar, garlic, onion, lime juice, brown sugar, Worcestershire sauce, Tabasco, and pepper, and heat the mixture to a boil. Lower the heat and simmer for about 10 minutes. Strain out the solids and discard them. Taste and adjust the seasonings.

» Heat the grill to high.

» Season the chicken with salt and pepper. When the grill is hot, place the chicken breasts on it, skin side down. Grill until done, turning several times. Just before removing from the heat, brush the sauce on the chicken and turn once or twice. Remove before it has a chance to burn.

» You can also try the sauce on steaks, as a sandwich topping, or as a dipping sauce for chicken nuggets—it makes a great all-around barbecue sauce.

Serves 4

Chicken with Tequila Lime Marinade

BE CAREFUL NOT TO OVER-MARINATE—the chicken will turn mushy. If you have any leftovers, slice them up and use for salad the next day.

» Whisk together the lime juice, tequila, olive oil, salt, pepper, and garlic. Pour this mixture over the chicken breasts in a glass dish. Cover and refrigerate 30 minutes, turning the chicken several times.

» Heat the grill to medium-high. Remove the chicken from the marinade, reserving the liquid. Cook chicken for about 8 minutes, turning frequently and basting with the reserved marinade until done.

Serves 6

....

Chicken Tostadas

TRY THIS SIMPLE WAY to cook chicken when you need a filling for enchiladas or burritos.

» Cover the fryer with water in a large pot, add the garlic and salt, and stew until the meat is cooked and tender, about one hour. Be careful not to overcook. Bone the chicken, shred the meat into bite-sized pieces, and set aside.

» Preheat oven to 350 degrees F.

» Fry the corn tortillas flat in hot oil in a large skillet until crisp and then let them drain on paper towels. Place them on a cookie sheet, spoon 2 tablespoons of shredded chicken onto each one, and top with grated cheese.

» Place the tostadas in the oven long enough to warm thoroughly and melt the cheese. Then top each tostada with olives, onions, lettuce, and tomatoes, and serve garnished with salsa, guacamole, or sour cream, or a combination.

Makes 12 tostadas

Grilled Fish with Roasted Tomato and Garlic Sauce

THIS RECIPE WAS INSPIRED BY FRESH GOLDEN TROUT, though snapper or any other mild fish would work well. Keeping the fish whole instead of cutting it into fillets helps maintain its moist and tender texture on the grill. It takes a few minutes longer to cook, but it's worth the wait.

» Preheat the oven to 425 degrees F.

» Line a baking sheet with parchment paper or aluminum foil. Place the tomatoes, onion, chiles, and garlic on the pan and place it in the oven. Roast, turning the vegetables several times, for about 15–20 minutes, until they are soft and beginning to brown. Set aside to cool.

» When the tomatoes and chiles are cool enough to handle, remove the cores, seeds, and skins. In a food processor or blender, pulse the roasted vegetables until a chunky sauce is formed. Add the cilantro, parsley, and salt. Taste and adjust the salt, if necessary. Set aside.

» Heat the grill to medium. Check the fish for any remaining scales and remove them as needed. Rinse well under running water and pat dry with paper towels. Rub the fish with oil, then sprinkle all over and inside with oregano, salt, and pepper.

» Place the fish directly on the preheated grill. Cook for about 6 minutes, then turn and cook another 6 minutes. When done, the fish will be flaky and opaque in the center—you can test it with a small paring knife.

» Serve the fish with the prepared tomato sauce and lime wedges. The sauce can be made a few days ahead and refrigerated. Bring it to room temperature before serving with the fish.

Serves 4

2 pounds ripe tomatoes

1 yellow or white onion, trimmed, peeled, and quartered

2 green chiles, preferably Hatch

8 cloves garlic

¼ cup fresh cilantro

3 tablespoons fresh flat-leaf parsley

1½ teaspoons kosher salt

1 whole, mild fish (3–4 pounds), head and scales removed, butterflied

¼ cup canola or olive oil

1–2 teaspoons oregano

Salt

Freshly ground black pepper

Lime wedges

Tangy Tuna Cabbage Salad

Tangy Tuna Cabbage Salad

¾ cup sliced red onion

3 tablespoons cider vinegar

1 can (12 ounces) organic albacore solid white tuna in olive oil or water, drained

¾ cup chopped Roma tomatoes

1 cup thinly sliced red bell pepper

3 cups sliced red cabbage

1 cup chopped fresh cilantro leaves, with a few tender stems

2–3 cups halved red seedless grapes

2 tablespoons extra-virgin olive oil

Salt

Freshly ground black pepper

1 whole Hass avocado

2 tablespoons Key lime juice

2 teaspoons Key lime zest

Cornhusk Salmon

12 dry cornhusks

1 cup dry white wine

Juice of 2 limes

¼ cup extra virgin olive oil

¼ teaspoon salt

1 teaspoon dried dill, or 1 tablespoon fresh

6 salmon fillets

2 limes, sliced

ALONG WITH MAKING A GORGEOUS PRESENTATION, this tasty one-dish meal is full of health-promoting foods.

» Soak the onion slices in the vinegar.

» In a large bowl, break up the tuna pieces into a flaky consistency. Add the marinated onion, including the vinegar, and toss. Gently mix in the tomatoes, bell pepper, cabbage, cilantro, and grapes. Pour olive oil over the salad and mix thoroughly, adding salt and pepper to taste. Place salad on individual plates.

» Slice, peel, and chop the avocado into bite-size pieces. Top off the salad with chopped avocado and sprinkle with lime juice and zest. Serve immediately, or if you want to chill the salad, hold the avocado and lime until it is served.

Serves 6

Cornhusk Salmon

THE SALMON FILLETS STEAM INSIDE THE CORNHUSKS, giving them a delightful, moist texture and a hint of smoky flavor.

» Soak the cornhusks in cold water until moist and pliable, about 1 hour.

» Whisk together the wine, lime juice, olive oil, salt, and dill, then pour this mixture over the salmon in a glass baking dish. Marinate for no more than 30 minutes, turning the fish once.

» Heat the grill to medium-high. Drain the cornhusks. For each serving, overlap 2 husks and place 1 salmon fillet in the middle. Cover the fish with lime slices, then wrap it in the husks and fasten with toothpicks.

» Place each fillet on the grill, then cover. Turn once, cooking approximately 4 minutes on each side, depending on the thickness of the fillets.

» Remove from the grill, place each fillet on a plate and open the husks with the lime side of the fish facing up.

Serves 6

TANGY TUNA
CABBAGE SALAD

Shrimp Mojo de Ajo

2 tablespoons unsalted butter, divided

1 pound shrimp (21–25 per pound), rinsed, shelled, and deveined

6 cloves garlic, minced

Juice of 1 lemon

¼ teaspoon oregano

½ teaspoon garlic-flavored Tabasco sauce

1 tablespoon finely chopped cilantro leaves

Pinch of salt

Pinch of freshly ground black pepper

MOJO DE AJO IS GARLIC SAUCE, which makes a magical combination with shrimp in this quick recipe. Use an oven-to-table baking dish for easy serving.

» Preheat the oven to 450 degrees F.

» Prepare a shallow pan or ovenproof baking dish by greasing it with half of the unsalted butter. Lay shrimp in one layer on the bottom of the baking dish.

» In a small bowl, mix the garlic, lemon juice, oregano, Tabasco, cilantro, salt, and pepper. Pour this mixture over the shrimp in the dish. Dot with the remaining butter.

» Place the baking dish in the oven and cook for about 5 minutes, or until the shrimp turn pink and opaque.

» Serve immediately with French bread for sopping up the leftover juices.

Serves 4

CORN & SQUASH

CORN AND SQUASH ARE TWO INVALUABLE CROPS grown in the Americas since agriculture began. Both corn and squash can be preserved by drying, canning, or freezing, which makes them accessible year-round, even when they're not in season. Winter squashes, with their hard rinds, will keep in a cool place for months, and their bright orange flesh adds some color to those dreary gray days of winter.

Of course, corn is best in the summer when it comes right out of the garden while it's still sweet and tender. You don't have to do much to it—bring a pot of water to a boil, add the ears of corn, and turn the heat off. Let it sit for about 5 minutes, and then drain, douse with butter and a little salt and pepper, and you have heaven.

To freeze corn, pick ears at the peak of freshness, rinse them well, and scrape the kernels from the cob with a sharp knife. Place them in a zippered plastic bag, squeeze out the air, and freeze for up to six months. Summer squash also freezes well. If you have an abundance of zucchini in your garden, grate it and freeze it. You can use it all winter in breads, casseroles, or even meatloaf.

Corn, above all, is a staple in Southwestern cooking. It shows up in breads, soups, tortillas, and in one of everyone's favorite comfort foods, tamales.

Basic Masa and Tamales

1 bag dried corn husks

2 pounds freshly ground masa for tamales, or 3 cups masa harina mixed with 2 cups warm water

1 cup fresh lard, at room temperature (page 105)

1½ teaspoons salt

1½ teaspoons baking powder

1½ cups homemade or low-sodium chicken stock

IF YOU LIVE NEAR A TORTILLERÍA or a large Latin American grocery store, you may be able to buy moist, freshly ground masa, which is ideal for making tamales. Be sure to ask for "masa para tamales" that has not already been mixed with lard or shortening, and find out whether or not it has already been salted. If so, omit the salt in the recipe. (If the store renders fresh lard, buy some of that, too!) Otherwise, you can make your own dough at home using masa harina and water.

Wherever you buy masa you should also be able to buy packages of hojas or dried corn husks for wrapping the tamales. Before use, clean the husks of any corn silk, cover them with water, and soak them until pliable. You will need some extra husks, as they tend to split, but narrow husks can easily be overlapped if necessary.

Tamales are traditionally steamed for about an hour in large enamelware pots, which you may also find for sale next to the husks and the masa. But you can use any steamer, or you can also pressure-cook them.

» Clean and soak the corn husks until they're softened and pliable.

» Meanwhile, if you're using masa harina, pour it into a bowl and add 2 cups warm water. Work the mixture into a dough with your hands, then set it aside to rest for about 15 minutes.

» Add the lard to the work bowl of a standing mixer fixed with the whisk attachment (or use a regular hand mixer in a large bowl) and beat it together with the salt and baking powder until light and fluffy.

» If you're using a stand mixer, switch to the paddle attachment. While beating, add the reconstituted or fresh masa by handfuls into the work bowl. Add the stock and beat until combined. Taste the mixture and add salt if necessary.

» Continue beating until the masa is light and fluffy, 15 to 20 minutes. The masa is ready when a grape-sized ball of dough floats in a glass of cold water. If the dough sinks, continue beating 5 minutes longer, then test it again.

» When the masa is ready, remove the corn husks from the water and set upright in a colander to let any remaining water drain.

» To make tamales, spread out the husk on a work surface, spread about ⅓ cup of masa down the center, and then add 1–2 tablespoons of any filling. Don't overfill; when the tamale is folded, the masa should enclose the filling. Fold over the sides and then either fold down the top and bottom and tie the tamale together with a strip of husk, or fold over the top of the husk, leaving one end open, and lay or prop the tamales fold sides down, to keep them closed until cooked.

» Stand the tamales in a steamer pot or pressure cooker with plenty of water in the bottom, at least two inches to prevent scorching. Steam for one hour or pressure cook for 40 minutes. Tamales are done when the masa has lost its pale floury color and has turned slightly golden and become somewhat firm. Remove from heat, keep covered, and allow to cool slightly. They continue to set as they cool.

» Serve hot with your favorite sauce. Be sure to provide an extra plate or bowl on the table for the discarded husks. Any leftovers may be frozen.

Makes enough for about
24 medium tamales

VARIATION *Vegetarian Masa*

ALTHOUGH LARD GIVES THE BEST RESULTS for tamales, you can also make a perfectly acceptable version using the same amount of palm oil or vegetable shortening. Under no circumstances should you try to use margarine for tamales; it simply will not work. Look for solid palm oil and other trans-fat-free shortenings at your natural foods store.

Grilled Corn with Compound Butter

Grilled Corn with Compound Butter

6 ears fresh corn, husks on

Compound butter (recipes follow)

Lime Cilantro Butter

1 stick unsalted butter, softened

2 tablespoons finely chopped fresh cilantro

1 shallot, finely chopped

1 teaspoon red chile powder

Garlic Lime Butter

1 stick unsalted butter, softened

4 cloves garlic, smashed

Juice and zest of 1 lime

1 teaspoon freshly ground black pepper

1 teaspoon kosher salt

Chipotle Butter

1 stick unsalted butter, softened

1 tablespoon chipotle powder

1 teaspoon sea salt

1 teaspoon ground cumin

1 teaspoon dried Mexican oregano

GRILLED CORN IS ONE OF THE FINEST summer pleasures. Probably the easiest way to cook it is also one of the tastiest; put it right on the grill, still in the husk. Compound butter is simply fresh butter with different combinations of spices and herbs added. You can be creative and experiment, or we offer a few options below.

» Peel back the cornhusks, but leave attached. If the ears have any stem left, leave it attached also. Remove the silk from the ears, rinse, and then wrap the husks back around the ears. Place in a pot of ice water for about 10 minutes.

» Preheat the grill to medium high heat.

» Drain the ears, pull the husks back and rub the kernels with softened compound butter. Replace the husks and then place the ears on the grill. Allow to cook until the husks are completely charred, about 10 minutes.

» Remove from the grill and serve immediately with more butter if so desired. Eat by peeling back the husks while holding on to the stem ends.

Serves 6

Lime Cilantro Butter

» In a bowl, combine the butter, cilantro, shallot, and chile powder.

Chipotle Butter

» In a small bowl, combine the butter, chipotle powder, salt, cumin, and oregano until well blended.

Garlic Lime Butter

» In a small bowl, combine the butter, garlic, lime juice and zest, pepper, and salt.

» Scrape the butter out onto a large piece of wax paper. Use the wax paper to roll the butter up into a log about 1½ inches in diameter. Chill until firm.

Makes ½ cup

RENDERING LARD

When the Great Fat Scare of the 1980s began, lard, which is rendered pork fat, fell out of favor because it was thought to be one big heart attack–inducing, cholesterol bomb. We now know that the trans-fat-laden shortenings and margarine that replaced it were much worse for our health, so lard is making a comeback. Avoid the processed stuff you find in the grocery store and ask your butcher to order it fresh for you.

If you can't find fresh lard, you can make it yourself. When you buy a pork shoulder or other fatty cut of pork, trim off as much fat as you can and set it aside. You can also ask the butcher for any pork trim he has, and he may just give it to you, rather than throw it away. The best lard comes from leaf fat, which comes from the abdominal cavity of the pig. If you know a farmer who raises hogs, ask if you can buy it when the animals are processed.

Once you have a pound or two of fat, grind it up or cut it into tiny cubes. Pour 1/4 cup of water into the bottom of a slow cooker and add the fat. Turn the heat to low. The fat will begin to melt. If it doesn't seem warm enough, turn the heat to high, but be careful. You don't want to burn any of the muscle meat that may still be left with the fat. Eventually all of the fat will be melted and the cracklings, those little pieces of meat, will be on the bottom. This can take up to several hours, depending on the amount of fat and the temperature of the slow cooker.

Ladle the fat into a colander lined with several layers of cheesecloth. After it's filtered and there are no more cracklings left, pour it into a glass jar to cool. Put the cracklings back into the slow cooker to get crispy and brown. They're good sprinkled on salad.

Store the lard in the refrigerator, where it will keep for several months. As with butter, just a little can take you a long way on the road to delicious.

Green Chile Chicken Tamales

2 cups shredded cooked chicken

1 recipe New Mexico Green Chile Sauce (page 47)

2 teaspoons dried Mexican oregano

Salt

Freshly ground black pepper

1 recipe Basic Masa (page 102)

At least 36 softened cornhusks (see above), plus 36 strips for tying (optional)

THIS IS AN EXTREMELY FLEXIBLE RECIPE. You'll need about 2 cups of shredded chicken, but it doesn't really matter where you get it—use grilled boneless skinless breasts, broiled thighs, or just pickings from a store-bought rotisserie chicken (one without any fancy seasonings, please). This recipe can easily be doubled or tripled. If you really like to smother your tamales with sauce, you should make a double batch of whichever sauce or salsa you choose.

» In a large bowl, combine the chicken and the chile sauce. Stir in the oregano, and add salt and pepper to taste.

» To assemble the tamales, spread about ⅓ cup of masa onto the center of each drained cornhusk. Spoon 1–2 tablespoons of the shredded chicken filling down the center of the dough. Fold up both ends and tie the tamale, or simply fold sides in and one end over to secure the masa inside; repeat with the remaining ingredients and cornhusks.

» Steam the tamales for 1 hour and serve with the remaining New Mexico Green Chile Sauce or Salsa Verde (page 52).

Makes about 24 tamales

Green Corn Tamales with Green Chile

THIS VERY TRADITIONAL DISH is a celebration of summer. In season, it is made with fresh white corn and fresh green chiles, and many aficionados work in groups and make huge batches because tamales, either cooked or raw, freeze perfectly for months. You must have the right kind of white tamale corn, not the eating ears sold in supermarkets. To make a big batch with fresh ingredients, it is also really necessary to have the corn ground commercially; for a small fee, some tortilla factories will do this for you.

The light, airy masa in the recipe below can be produced year-round and is made with grits and, ideally, with fresh ears of corn. The green cornhusks are used to wrap the tamales. If fresh corn is out of season, you can make a version that's almost as good with frozen corn and dried husks. If you prefer a milder tamale, you can omit the green chiles. And try a little cheese in the middle too, if you like.

» If you are using fresh corn, remove the husks, discarding the silks, and set the husks aside. Keep them covered so they don't dry out.

» Slice the corn kernels from the cobs, being careful to collect all of the juices.

» In a large skillet over medium heat, melt the butter. Add the onion and garlic and sauté until softened. Add the green chiles, corn and its juices, and heavy cream; cook, stirring, about 5 minutes.

» Remove the pan from the heat and stir in the baking powder and grits. Season to taste with salt.

» Tear 16 strips from the fresh corn leaves, if you're using them.

» To assemble the tamales, spread about ¼ cup masa in the middle of a corn husk. If you wish, fill with a strip or two of chile and a tablespoon of cheese. Fold up both ends and tie the tamale, or simply fold one end over; repeat with the remaining ingredients and cornhusks.

» Steam the tamales for 1 hour and serve plain, or with the salsa of your choice.

Makes 12 tamales

10 ears fresh corn (or about 6 cups frozen corn)

3 tablespoons unsalted butter

½ small white onion, diced

2 cloves garlic, minced

1 cup roasted, peeled, and chopped green chiles (page 32)

½ cup heavy cream

½ teaspoon baking powder

½ cup grits (uncooked)

Salt

16 softened cornhusks, plus 16 optional strips for tying (if you're not using fresh corn)

Shredded green chile for filling (optional)

Grated longhorn cheddar cheese for filling (optional)

Salsa of your choice, for serving

Pork and Red Chile Tamales

2½ pounds boneless pork butt, trimmed of excess fat

6 cloves garlic, peeled

1 teaspoon black peppercorns

2 bay leaves

1 teaspoon salt

Water

1 recipe New Mexico Red Chile Sauce (page 46)

1 recipe Basic Masa (page 102)

At least 36 softened cornhusks, plus 36 strips for tying (optional)

THESE ARE SOME OF THE MOST COMMON TAMALES in the Southwest. They can be found in restaurants, cafés, and in the coolers toted by strolling vendors. Everybody loves them, so make a bunch and freeze any leftovers. This recipe makes enough pork filling to make another batch of tamales, but you can always use the extra pork for burritos or freeze it for later use. In some families it's traditional to put a single stuffed green olive in each of these tamales.

» Arrange the pork butt in a large Dutch oven. Add the garlic, peppercorns, bay leaves, and salt. Add enough cold water to cover by several inches. Bring the liquid to a boil, then reduce the heat and simmer, partially covered, for about 2 hours.

» Transfer the pork to a cutting board and allow it to rest 20 minutes. Using two forks, shred the meat. In a bowl, combine 2 cups of the shredded pork with enough New Mexico Red Chile Sauce to thoroughly moisten the meat.

» To assemble the tamales, spread about ⅓ cup masa onto the center of each cornhusk. Spoon 1–2 tablespoons of the shredded pork filling down the center of the dough. Fold up both ends and tie the tamale, or simply fold one end over; repeat with the remaining ingredients and cornhusks.

» Steam the tamales for 1 hour and serve smothered with the remaining New Mexico Red Chile Sauce.

Makes about 24 tamales

Calabacitas

4 tablespoons butter

½ cup chopped onion

2 small zucchini (about ½ pound), diced

2 small yellow summer squash (about ½ pound), diced

Approximately 1½ cups corn kernels (about 2 large ears)

2 New Mexico or Anaheim green chiles, roasted, peeled, seeded, and chopped (page 2)

Salt

1 cup shredded Monterey Jack or cheddar cheese

½ cup chopped fresh cilantro

MAKE THIS DISH IN THE LATE SUMMER when corn, squash, and chiles are all found at farmers markets and roadside stands. You can use one kind of squash or a combination, and you can also wrap these calabacitas up into vegetarian burritos.

» In a large skillet over medium heat, melt the butter. Add the onion, zucchini, and summer squash, and cook for 5 minutes. Add the corn and green chiles, and continue cooking until the zucchini and summer squash are tender. Add salt to taste.

» Remove from heat, toss with cheese and cilantro, and serve hot.

Serves 4–6

Red Chile Pork Posole

2 cups dried hominy (or 2 large cans hominy)

1 large onion, diced, plus 1 cup diced for garnish

1 tablespoon finely chopped garlic

2 tablespoons olive oil or lard

1 pound pork stew meat

2 dried New Mexico chile pods, stemmed, seeded, and chopped

¼ teaspoon ground cloves

1 teaspoon salt

½ cup finely chopped fresh cilantro, for garnish

HERE IS SOME REAL SOUTHWESTERN COMFORT FOOD. Make it when you'll be home all day and are expecting a crowd for dinner. You can substitute canned hominy for dried posole (it's the same thing and is often sold in the Southwest as nixtamal), but canned hominy can be a bit soggy, so add it later. Serve with warm flour tortillas on the side.

» Put the dried hominy in a large bowl and cover with plenty of lightly salted water. Allow to soak overnight.

» In a large stockpot, sauté the onions and garlic in oil or lard. Add the pork in batches and cook until the cubes are browned on all sides. Remove the meat from the pot and set aside.

» Place into the same pot the chiles, cloves, salt, drained hominy, and enough water to cover. Bring to a boil, then reduce heat to low and simmer at least 3 hours, or until the hominy kernels are puffy and tender. If you are using canned hominy, drain and add it after 2 hours. Add more water if necessary.

» Add the cooked pork and cook 30 minutes longer.

» Serve hot and garnish with cilantro and onion.

Serves 8–10

Menudo

2 calf's feet, or pig trotters, whichever you can find

5 pounds tripe

3 cups nixtamal, or two large cans hominy

4 cloves garlic, chopped

2 medium onions, chopped fine

6 quarts water

1½ tablespoons salt

1 tablespoon dried Mexican oregano

2 lemons or 4 limes, cut into small wedges, for garnish

Crushed chile pequín, for garnish

Sliced green onions, for garnish

4 cups New Mexico Red Chile Sauce (page 46), warmed, for garnish

MENUDO IS THE TRADITIONAL DISH served on New Year's Eve and is said to bring good luck for the year ahead. It's also a traditional remedy for a hangover!

» Clean the calf's feet or trotters well, cover with cold water in a large stockpot, and simmer for 1½ hours, skimming the foam from the pot as necessary.

» Meanwhile, soak the tripe for about an hour, changing the water several times, and then wash thoroughly and cut into 1-inch squares.

» Wash the nixtamal thoroughly to remove any trace of lime.

» When the feet are finished cooking, remove from the pot, cool slightly, and then remove the meat, discarding the bones. Chop the meat into small pieces. Return to the pot.

» Add the tripe, nixtamal, garlic, and onions to the pot and cover with an additional 6 quarts of water. If you're using canned hominy, wait to add it until the last hour of cooking. Bring to a boil and skim any foam or residue from the top of the pot. Reduce heat, cover, and simmer for about 6 hours. Add the salt and oregano and simmer uncovered for another half hour.

» Remove from heat and adjust the salt, if necessary.

» Serve in deep bowls with the lemon and lime wedges, chile pequín, and green onions. Add a healthy dollop of red chile sauce to the bowl, if desired.

Serves 18–20

Chile Corn Chowder

SOUPS AND STEWS ARE PERFECT DISHES for showcasing chiles, where their heat can permeate every spoonful. But it is the more subtle ingredients—in this case, sweet corn and milk—that serve as a foil for the chile's potential sting and make a chile-infused chowder very special.

» Cut the corn kernels from the cobs and set aside. Break the cobs in half, place them in a 1½-quart saucepan with the milk, and bring to a simmer over medium heat. Do not scald the milk. After it comes to a simmer, remove the milk from the heat and allow to steep for 30 minutes. Strain, discarding all the solids. Set aside.

» In a stockpot, heat the oil. Add the bacon and cook until crisp. Remove the bacon and allow it to drain on a plate covered with a paper towel. Add the onion to the bacon fat, sautéing until tender. Add the celery and potato; sauté for 2 minutes. Add the stock and bring to a boil over medium-high heat. Reduce heat and simmer until the potatoes are cooked through.

» Add the milk infusion, corn kernels, bacon, lime zest, diced poblano, and diced red pepper. Simmer until heated through. Add the lime juice, then season to taste with salt, pepper, and Tabasco sauce. Serve hot, garnished with a sprinkling of grated pepper Jack cheese and thinly sliced scallion greens.

4 servings

---

2 ears of corn, shucked and cleaned

2 cups whole milk

2 teaspoons olive oil

4 pieces of thick-sliced bacon, diced

½ cup diced onion

1 stalk celery, diced

1 russet potato, peeled and diced small

2 cups chicken or vegetable stock

Zest of 1 lime

1 poblano, roasted, peeled, seeded, and diced small

¼ cup small diced red bell pepper

1 tablespoon fresh lime juice

Salt

Freshly ground black pepper

Tabasco sauce

Grated pepper Jack cheese, for garnish

Thinly sliced scallion tops (green parts), for garnish

Corn Bisque with Garlic and Chiles

2 tablespoons unsalted butter

1 cup chopped yellow onions

4 cloves garlic, minced

½ cup chopped green chile

¼ cup diced carrot

¼ cup diced celery

¼ cup diced red bell pepper

4 cups fresh or frozen corn kernels, thawed and drained

¼ teaspoon cayenne

3 cups chicken stock

½ cup half-and-half or whole milk

Freshly ground black pepper

Salt

FEEL FREE TO ADD YOUR OWN TOUCH to this bisque, whether it's celery or a variety of chiles. It's a versatile recipe that responds well to experimentation.

» Melt the butter in a large saucepan over medium-high heat. Add onions, garlic, chile, carrot, celery, and red bell pepper, and sauté for about 3 minutes. Add 3 cups of the corn and the cayenne, and sauté another 2 minutes or so. Add the stock and bring the mixture to a boil. Reduce heat and simmer uncovered until the vegetables are tender and the liquid is slightly reduced, about 30 minutes.

» Working in batches, puree the soup in a blender (or use a stick blender). Return the soup to the pot. Mix in the half-and-half and the remaining cup of corn. Season to taste with salt and pepper.

» This can be prepared a day ahead. Cover and refrigerate. Reheat before serving.

Serves 4

Squash and Black Bean Soup

1 small butternut squash

1 tablespoon butter

5 cups cooked black beans, rinsed and drained

1 cup drained canned tomatoes, chopped

¼ cup unsalted butter

1 medium onion, chopped

5 shallots, minced

4 garlic cloves, minced

2 tablespoons ground cumin

1 teaspoon salt

½ teaspoon freshly ground black pepper

4 cups beef stock

½ cup dry sherry

½ pound cooked ham, cut into ⅛-inch dice

3 to 4 tablespoons sherry vinegar

Sour cream and coarsely chopped pepitas for garnish

ON THOSE FALL NIGHTS WHEN THERE'S A NIP IN THE AIR, there's nothing better than a big pot of soup. This one is rich and filling, and the addition of sherry makes it mellow. For a vegetarian version, omit the ham and trade the beef stock for vegetable.

» Heat the oven to 425 degrees F.

» Cut the butternut squash in half lengthwise and scrape out the seeds. Coat the flesh with butter and place skin-side up on a baking sheet. Bake for 30–40 minutes or until the flesh is tender. Remove from the oven and set aside to cool.

» Place 4 cups of beans and all of the tomatoes into a food processor. Puree until coarsely chopped.

» When the squash is cool enough to handle, scrape the flesh away from the skin and add to the bean puree in the food processor. Process until the mixture is fairly smooth. You may have to do this in two batches.

» Place a stockpot over medium-high heat and add the butter. When it's melted, add the onion, shallots, garlic, cumin, salt, and pepper, stirring until onion is softened and beginning to brown. Stir in the bean/squash puree, the stock, and sherry until combined. Simmer, uncovered, stirring occasionally for 25 minutes, or until thick enough to coat the back of a spoon. Just before serving, add the remaining one cup of beans, ham, and vinegar, and simmer the soup, stirring, until heated through. Season with salt and pepper to taste. Serve garnished with a dollop of sour cream and a sprinkle of pepitas.

Serves 6

Southwest Corn Bread

THIS IS SO RICH AND TASTY it could almost be a meal in itself, but it's even better served as part of a Southwestern buffet.

» Preheat oven to 400 degrees F. Spray a 9 x 13 x 2-inch pan with cooking spray.

» In a large bowl, combine the cornmeal, sugar, salt, flour, and baking powder. Make a well in the center and add the egg, milk, and oil. Stir until moistened, leaving lumps. Add creamed corn and cottage cheese, stirring until blended. Avoid the tendency to overmix. Lumps are acceptable.

» Pour one half of batter into prepared pan. Cover with green chiles and cheese. Top with remaining batter. Bake one hour or until top is golden brown and a knife inserted in the center comes out clean. Remove from the oven and cool on a wire rack for ten minutes, then slice into 3-inch squares and remove from pan.

Makes 16 servings

1 cup yellow cornmeal

¼ cup sugar

1 teaspoon salt

1 cup flour

3 teaspoons baking powder

1 egg, lightly beaten

1 cup milk

¼ cup canola oil

1 can (14½-ounce) creamed corn

1 cup cottage cheese

1 cup green chiles, roasted, peeled, seeded, and chopped

1 cup grated cheddar cheese

Blue Corn Blueberry Pancakes

2 large eggs

1½–2 cups milk or buttermilk

1 cup blue cornmeal

1 cup all-purpose flour

1 tablespoon baking powder

1 tablespoon sugar

½ teaspoon salt

6 tablespoons butter, melted

Oil or cooking spray

1 cup fresh blueberries, plus more for serving

CORN COMES IN MANY COLORS besides yellow, including red, pink, white, and black. Blue corn is a favorite of Pueblo and Hispanic cooks in northern Arizona and New Mexico, particularly for tortillas. Now available in many supermarkets, blue cornmeal is interchangeable with standard yellow. You'll taste the same corny flavor, but the color—especially when deepened with blueberries—is unique. This easy blue recipe is adapted from a popular breakfast treat served at the historic Arizona Inn in Tucson.

» In a small bowl, beat the eggs with 1½ cups milk or buttermilk.

» In a medium bowl, whisk together the cornmeal, flour, baking powder, sugar, and salt. Blend in milk and eggs, then whisk in butter. Add more milk if the batter seems too thick.

» Heat a griddle or skillet over medium heat. When it's hot enough to make a drop of water sizzle, grease the griddle lightly with oil or spray. Ladle the batter onto the griddle in ¼- to ⅓-cup portions, and quickly dot each pancake with about 6 blueberries. Cook until the bottoms of the pancakes are golden brown, then turn and finish baking (about 4 minutes in all).

» Serve hot with additional berries and warm syrup.

Makes 10–12 pancakes

CITRUS & OTHER FRUIT

THE SOUTHWEST is known for its abundance of fruit-growing regions. From the citrus groves of Arizona and Texas, to the apple and cherry orchards of New Mexico and the avocados, peaches, melons, and grapes of Southern California, fresh fruit is a vital part of Southwest cuisine, and valued for its zest and sourness as well as its sweetness.

The acidity of citrus lends itself well to brightening the flavor of soups and stews, and it plays an important role in marinades, especially when making ceviche, which is seafood "cooked" in citrus juice. Oranges, tangerines, lemons, limes, and grapefruit are all enjoyed in both sweet and spicy dishes, as well as on their own.

And then there are the exotic indigenous fruits. Prickly pear fruit is both earthy and sweet, and can be turned into syrup or preserves. Tamarind is a leguminous fruit that comes from a tree native to Africa, but it grows throughout the tropics and can be found all over Mexico. If you have trouble finding the pods, you can also find tamarind paste in Asian or Mexican groceries. It's used in savory dishes and is also a popular flavoring for drinks and sauces.

Let's not forget the pomegranate—the round, heavy fruit with the jewel-like, crunchy garnet seeds, brought to the New World by the Spaniards. You'll find pomegranate seeds sprinkled on salads, adding a pleasing crunch and color to salsas, or juiced and added to everything from barbecue sauces to jams, jellies, and drinks.

Perhaps because of the spices and complex flavors involved in Southwest cuisine, fruit is a traditional way to end a meal.

Agua Fresca de Melón o Sandía (Cantaloupe or Watermelon Drink)

Agua Fresca de Melón o Sandía

4 cups cubed cantaloupe or watermelon

¼ cup Key lime juice

1 tablespoon evaporated cane juice or honey

4 cups water, divided

Lime slices

Ice

FOR GENERATIONS, STREET VENDORS THROUGHOUT MEXICO have enticed passersby with glistening barrel-shaped glass jugs filled with colorful iced aguas frescas ("fresh waters"). These drinks rely on the sweetness of the fruit rather than the overpowering sweetness of sugar. Flavors are limitless. With a dash of creativity it's easy to make your own signature aguas frescas.

» Blend the melon pieces, lime juice, evaporated cane juice, and ½ cup of the water. Pour over a coarse strainer into a pitcher; then stir in the remaining water. Serve over ice in a tall glass and garnish with a lime slice. For a thicker drink with more fiber, don't strain.

Serves 4

VARIATION

Agua Fresca de Tamarindo

Agua Fresca de Tamarindo

8–12 cups water, divided

6–8 tamarind pods

1 cinnamon stick

1 teaspoon pure vanilla extract

1–2 tablespoons honey

BOILED TAMARIND PODS ARE TART and carry an earthy undertone; thus this drink is often made very sweet. Vanilla, a cinnamon stick, and a little sweetener create a tasty, cola-like balance of flavors. Also, it loses some of its sourness after it sits in the fridge for a couple hours. If you can't find pods, you can use tamarind paste. Soak a golf-ball-size piece in hot water with a cinnamon stick for about 20 minutes or until it's soft, and then follow the directions below.

» In a small saucepan, bring 2 cups of the water, the pods, and the cinnamon stick to a boil. Reduce heat and simmer for about 20 minutes; then turn off heat and steep for about two hours or until pulp softens. When cooled, remove the hard shell and root-looking pieces and discard them. Press the seeds and pulp against a fine sieve, forcing the juice through and into a half-gallon pitcher. Add vanilla, honey, and the remaining 6–10 cups of water (use the amount of water needed to achieve the desired strength). Serve over ice. This drink may be stored in the refrigerator for a day or two.

Serves 6-8

Jalapeño Limeade

AN AMERICAN TAKE ON THE AGUAS FRESCAS so popular in Mexican marketplaces, this is a refreshing summer sip with just a hint of a kick.

» In a 1-quart saucepan, combine the sugar and 1 cup of water. Bring the mixture to a boil over medium-high heat. Add the jalapeños, reduce the heat, and simmer for 5 minutes. Cool thoroughly; strain out the jalapeños.

» In a half-gallon jug or pitcher filled halfway with ice, combine the fresh lime juice with the sugar syrup. Top off with enough water to fill the container. You can adjust the flavor with honey or more lime juice.

Makes ½ gallon

1 cup sugar

1 cup water

2 jalapeños, split in half

1 cup fresh lime juice

Ice

Honey, optional

Prickly Pear Lemonade

Prickly Pear Lemonade

3 cups fresh lemon juice

4 cups water

1 cup superfine sugar

¼–½ cup prickly pear syrup (recipe follows)

Lemon wedges and sugar for glass rims

Chilled club soda

Mint leaves, for garnish

Prickly Pear Syrup

12 medium prickly pear fruits

Juice of 1 lemon

1½ cups sugar

1 teaspoon cornstarch (optional)

PRICKLY PEAR SYRUP COMES FROM THE FRUIT of the prickly pear cactus. If you're lucky enough to have prickly pear in your yard, you can harvest the fruit and make it yourself. If not, you can find it at some specialty food stores or order it online.

» Combine the lemon juice, water, cup of sugar, and prickly pear syrup in a large pitcher. Rub the rim of each glass with a lemon wedge, then roll in sugar to coat. Add ice cubes to each glass, fill about ¾ full with lemonade mixture, then top off with club soda. Garnish each serving with a lemon wedge and mint leaves.

Serves 6

Prickly Pear Syrup

» Put the prickly pear fruit in a bowl or dishpan full of water. Holding each one with tongs, scrub with a vegetable brush to remove dust and some of the stickers (the rest will come out later when you strain the juice). Transfer 6 at a time to a blender jar and process until liquid. Line a mesh strainer with cheesecloth and strain juice into a medium saucepan. You should have about 1 cup. Add the lemon juice and sugar and slowly bring to a simmer. Cook until the syrup begins to thicken. If you want a thicker syrup, stir in the cornstarch dissolved in a little cold water and cook to thicken. Stir with wire whisk if necessary to smooth consistency. (Adding dry cornstarch to hot liquid will result in lumps.)

Makes about 1 pint

Chile-Spiced Grilled Fruit

¼ cup canola oil

1 tablespoon citrus juice

1 serrano chile, chopped (with seeds and ribs)

¼ vanilla bean pod

1 teaspoon salt

¼ teaspoon chile powder

1 teaspoon sugar

4 serving-size pieces of fresh, ripe fruits (for example, 2 large peaches, cut in half; 4 slices of pineapple, 1 inch thick; 4 bananas, peeled and cut in half lengthwise; or 2 pears, halved and cored)

THE TINGLE OF CHILES ADDS AN ENTICING TASTE sensation to the smoky sweetness of grilled ripe fruit. This recipe can serve as a sweet/savory side dish for your favorite grilled meats and it also becomes a satisfying dessert when served with ice cream or biscotti.

» If your grill is not already hot from preparing the main course, heat it to medium-low. If the grates are dirty from use, clean them or cover them with aluminum foil.

» Combine the oil, juice, and chopped chile; scrape the vanilla bean seeds into the mixture, then include the pod. Allow to sit for 10 minutes.

» Combine the salt, chile powder, and sugar; set aside.

» Set the fruit on a baking pan or large plate. Brush generously with the marinade mixture on all sides. Allow to sit for 5 minutes. Also brush the grill grates or aluminum foil with some of the marinade.

» If grilling directly on the grates, brush off some of the marinade to prevent flare-ups.

» Season the fruit pieces with the salt mixture.

» Gently place the fruit, cut side down, on the grill. Do not move it for at least 2 minutes. Cooking time will depend on the texture of the fruit. Turn it over when dark golden grill marks are visible. Continue to cook until the fruit is soft and heated through. Use a spatula to gently remove the fruit from the grill.

Serves 4

Jicama Pineapple Salad

THIS SWEET AND SLIGHTLY PIQUANT SALAD would also work well as a salsa to serve with grilled chicken or fish. Or just add chips and you've got an appetizer.

» Whisk together the oil, vinegar, garlic, cilantro, and cumin in a small bowl to blend. Season with salt and pepper to taste.

» Combine jicama and pineapple in a bowl and toss with just enough dressing to coat evenly.

Serves 4

▲▲▲▲▲▲▲▲▲▲▲▲▲▲▲▲▲▲▲▲

JICAMA

Jicama resembles a large, beige turnip, sometimes covered in a waxy coating to extend the shelf life. But inside that drab exterior lives a sweet taste and crunchy texture. The smaller and heavier they are, the better the flavor.

To serve, use a knife to remove the peel and slice the jicama into strips. Sprinkle with some lime juice and then dust with chile powder, cayenne pepper, and salt for a quick appetizer.

You can also add jicama to a salad. Arrange red and green bell peppers, fresh orange slices, Kalamata olives, and jicama over a bed of red leaf lettuce and drizzle it with olive oil and balsamic vinegar. Finish with a sprinkle of flaky sea salt and freshly ground black pepper. Serve it as a side or starter with your favorite grilled steak.

▼▼▼▼▼▼▼▼▼▼▼▼▼▼▼▼▼▼▼▼

⅓ cup canola oil

3 tablespoons white wine vinegar or sherry vinegar

1 tablespoon minced garlic

¼ cup chopped fresh cilantro leaves

¼ teaspoon ground cumin

Salt

Freshly ground black pepper

1 small jicama, grated with largest holes of grater

1 cup diced fresh pineapple

Ceviche

½ pound fresh medium shrimp, peeled and deveined

½ pound fresh medium scallops

½ pound firm white fish, skinned and cut into 1-inch chunks

1 cup fresh lime juice

⅓ cup chopped red onion

2 tomatoes, finely chopped

2 fresh jalapeños, seeds and ribs removed, finely chopped

½ yellow pepper, finely chopped

1 avocado, finely chopped

½ cup extra virgin olive oil

1 tablespoon minced cilantro

1 clove garlic, minced

½ teaspoon salt

¼ teaspoon freshly ground black pepper

1 teaspoon red pepper flakes

2 bay leaves

THIS RECIPE WILL MAKE YOU THINK OF HAPPY TIMES on the beach in Mexico, sitting under a shady palapa with a cold Pacifico and a platter of fish "cooked" in lime juice–even if you've never gone south of the border. Here the presentation is a little more refined, but the spirit is still there. Use the freshest seafood you can find, and don't forget the cerveza!

» Combine the shrimp, scallops, and fish in a glass dish; then cover them with lime juice. Refrigerate for 8 hours.

» Drain the seafood mixture and combine with the red onion, tomatoes, jalapeños, yellow pepper, and avocado.

» Whisk together the olive oil, cilantro, garlic, salt, pepper, and red pepper flakes in a small bowl; add the bay leaves after whisking. Pour this over the fish mixture and refrigerate for 1 hour.

» Drain the ceviche and remove the bay leaves.

» For each serving, line a stemmed glass with lettuce leaves, then spoon in some ceviche. Garnish with a sprig of cilantro and a wedge of lime, and serve with a basket of hot tortilla chips (page 10).

Serves 6

Garlic Roasted Asparagus with Orange Zest

Cooking spray (optional)

1 pound asparagus, trimmed

2 tablespoons olive oil

6 cloves garlic, minced

Shredded peel from 1 large navel orange

HERE'S AN EXQUISITE COMBINATION of beauty and flavor. Zest is the colored part of the fruit rind that contains flavorful and aromatic citrus oil. The best way to remove the zest without getting any of the underlying bitter white membrane is with a Microplane grater or a citrus zester, or by rubbing the fruit over the fine holes of a box grater, being careful not to include any of the pith.

» Preheat the oven to 425 degrees F.

» Prepare a jelly-roll pan or a rimmed cookie sheet by coating it with nonstick baking spray, or line the pan with parchment paper.

» Place the asparagus on the prepared pan and drizzle it with olive oil. Sprinkle it evenly with garlic and shredded orange peel. Place the pan in the oven and bake for 5 minutes. Remove the pan from the oven and roll the asparagus over, using tongs. Return the pan to the oven and bake until done, about 3–5 minutes. The asparagus will be tender and just beginning to darken.

Serves 6

Lemon Chicken Topopo

4 boneless, skinless chicken breasts

2 cups water

Juice of 1 lemon

½ teaspoon salt

¼ teaspoon white pepper

1 teaspoon red pepper flakes

½ cup vegetable oil

4 corn tortillas

1 (14 ounce) can black beans, drained and rinsed

8 cups shredded romaine lettuce

2 avocados, peeled, seeded, and sliced lengthwise

2 large tomatoes, cut into wedges

2 small (2 ounce) cans sliced black olives

1 bunch green onions

1 cup crumbled queso fresco or feta cheese

Lemon Vinaigrette Dressing (recipe follows)

THIS IS A SLIGHTLY DIFFERENT TWIST on the traditional topopo or tostada salad that you'll find on restaurant menus.

» Place the chicken breasts in a deep skillet and cover with the water. Add the lemon juice, salt, pepper, and red pepper flakes. Cover and bring to a simmer, poaching gently until the chicken is cooked, about 25 minutes. Cool, then slice across the grain into strips. (This can be prepared 1 day ahead.)

» Heat the oil in a deep skillet, and then fry the tortillas, one at a time, until crisp. Drain them well on paper towels.

» To assemble the salads, place a tortilla in the middle of each of 4 plates, then top each one with black beans. Add a mound of lettuce, then arrange the sliced chicken, avocado, tomato wedges, black olives, green onions, and queso fresco on top of each. Drizzle with Lemon Vinaigrette Dressing.

Serves 4

Lemon Vinaigrette Dressing

» Whisk ingredients together in a small bowl. Serve immediately.

Makes 1 cup

Roasted Chicken with Cilantro-Lime Rub

WITH THE UBIQUITY OF ROTISSERIE CHICKENS in supermarkets, it is tempting to give up roasting your own. Resist the urge. Especially if you can use a locally raised chicken, the results far surpass supermarket birds.

» Preheat the oven to 425 degrees F.

» Rinse the chicken with cold water, then pat it dry, and remove any excess fat. Sprinkle salt and pepper on the inside and outside of the bird.

» In a bowl, combine the cilantro, garlic, red pepper flakes, lime juice, and 2 tablespoons of the olive oil.

» Use your hand to gently separate the chicken skin from the breast and thighs. Spread the cilantro paste between the skin and the meat. Spread the remaining tablespoon of olive oil over the outside of the chicken.

» Place the chicken on a rack in a roasting pan. Roast about 1 hour, or until the skin is golden brown and the temperature of the thickest part of the thigh is 165 degrees F.

» Remove the chicken from the oven, tent loosely with foil and allow to rest about 15 minutes.

» Carve and serve with pan juices.

Serves 2-4

Lemon Vinaigrette Dressing

½ cup extra virgin olive oil

3 tablespoons white wine vinegar

1 tablespoon fresh lemon juice

1 clove garlic, smashed

1 small fresh jalapeño, seeded and finely chopped

1 tablespoon fresh parsley, finely minced

¼ teaspoon salt

Roasted Chicken with Cilantro-Lime Rub

1 roasting chicken

Salt

Freshly ground black pepper

⅓ cup chopped cilantro

3 cloves garlic, finely chopped

½ teaspoon red pepper flakes

Juice of ½ lime

3 tablespoons olive oil

DESSERTS

DESSERT IS USUALLY SIMPLE IN SOUTHWEST CUISINE—fresh fruit, cookies, or ice cream are all common ends to a satisfying meal. But on special occasions, when families and friends gather, the desserts become more complex. Flan (a Southwestern version of crème caramel), cakes, and custard desserts are all a part of everything from baby showers and birthday parties to graduations and weddings.

Chocolate, with its origins in Mexico and Central America, is a favorite ingredient. When cooking with chocolate, it's important to understand the various types and what they add to a recipe.

Bittersweet, semisweet, or dark chocolate In the United States, dark chocolate must contain no milk powder and a minimum of 35% cocoa solids. Better brands contain a higher percentage. The percentage of sugar usually determines whether a bar is bittersweet or semisweet.

Chocolate chips Designed to hold their shape during the baking process, chocolate chips come in milk, dark, and white chocolate. Because they have a different cocoa butter content, they aren't a great replacement for bar chocolate when cooking or baking.

Cocoa powder The pulverized solid left after the cocoa butter is removed from chocolate liquor, it can be used as a seasoning in savory dishes or to add chocolaty richness to desserts. Natural cocoa is simply pulverized; Dutch cocoa has been treated to neutralize the slight acidity of the natural powder.

Mexican chocolate Very sweet and flavored with cinnamon, Mexican chocolate comes in tablets that should be grated before using. It's not good to eat by itself because it's gritty due to the high granulated sugar content. Ibarra and Abuelita are popular brands found in many grocery stores.

Biscochitos

6–8 cups all-purpose flour

5 teaspoons baking powder

Salt

1¾ cups white sugar, plus 5
    teaspoons

1 cup brown sugar

2 cups butter, lard, or shortening

4 eggs

1 cup milk

2 teaspoons anise seeds (or more if
    you like the flavor)

¾ cup water

2½ teaspoons cinnamon

THE BISCOCHITO (ALSO SPELLED BIZCOCHITO) IS THE OFFICIAL STATE COOKIE of New Mexico. These excellent confections, delicately spiced and not too sweet, are essential to many holidays, usually making their appearance right after Thanksgiving to be shared as gifts or stored away for holiday parties later. Either lard, which is traditional, or butter will make a much tastier cookie than shortening.

» Preheat the oven to 350 degrees F.

» Sift or whisk 6 cups of the flour with the baking powder and a big pinch of salt, and set aside.

» Cream together 1¾ cups of white sugar and the brown sugar with the butter. Add the eggs and milk and mix well.

» Meanwhile, simmer the anise for 10 minutes in the water and then stir it into the sugar, fat, and egg mixture. Gradually add the sifted flour mixture.

» Prepare the rolling surface and pastry rolling pin with a light dusting of flour. Be careful because too much flour will toughen the dough. Roll out the dough approximately ¼ inch thick and cut with a cookie cutter. A 3-inch size is best, and let the shape be dictated by the occasion. Easter eggs are just as welcome as hearts or stars, depending on the season. In Santa Fe, a fleur-de-lis shape is popular.

» Mix the remaining sugar with the cinnamon and dust the cookies with the mixture. Transfer them to a cookie sheet and bake for about 10 minutes. Watch them carefully and be ready to remove them when they reach an even, delicate brown. They keep well.

Makes 6 dozen cookies

Piñon Cookies

THESE WILL REMIND YOU OF THE SUGAR COOKIES known as "tea cakes," but with a Southwestern flair. Try to find local or European pine nuts if you can, even if it means shelling them yourself. The nuts imported from China have been associated with health problems in the United States.

» Preheat the oven to 300 degrees F.

» Line 2 baking sheets with parchment paper.

» In a food processor fitted with a metal blade, place the almond paste (breaking it up into small pieces), sugar, powdered sugar, and flour. Pulse several times until the mixture is finely ground. Add the egg whites a little at a time, just until the dough comes together. You may or may not need all of the egg whites, depending on the moisture content of the almond paste and other ingredients. Remove the blade from the food processor.

» Place the piñons in a shallow dish. With a spoon and damp hands, scoop a small amount of dough, roll it into a ball, and roll it in the piñons until it is lightly coated. Place the cookie on a prepared cookie sheet. Repeat until all the dough is used, placing the cookies about 2 inches apart.

» Place the baking sheets in the oven and bake for 20–25 minutes, or until the cookies are firm. Remove the cookies from the sheets using a thin spatula and let them cool on wire racks. Dust with powdered sugar immediately before serving.

Makes 2 dozen

1 can (8 ounces) almond paste

½ cup sugar

½ cup powdered sugar, plus more for garnish

¼ cup all-purpose flour

2 large egg whites, lightly beaten

1 cup piñon nuts

Chocolate Pumpkin Empanadas

3 cups flour

2 teaspoons baking powder

3 tablespoons sugar, plus ¼ cup

½ teaspoon salt

½ cup butter, very cold and cut into pieces

¼ cup milk

1 can (15 ounces) pumpkin (not pie filling)

1 can (14 ounces) sweetened condensed milk

1 egg

1 teaspoon ground cinnamon

½ teaspoon ground ginger

½ teaspoon ground nutmeg

8 ounces premium dark chocolate, broken into 16 uniform pieces

1 egg, beaten

PUMPKIN EMPANADAS ARE A WELL-LOVED PASTRY of Mexico and the Southwest. Adding a little chocolate turns them into a super comfort food.

» Sift together the flour, baking powder, 3 tablespoons sugar, and salt. Cut in the butter until the mixture resembles coarse meal. Add the milk, a tablespoon at a time, until the dough is soft and holds together. Wrap the dough in plastic and refrigerate for 30 minutes.

» Preheat the oven to 350 degrees F.

» In a large bowl, combine the pumpkin, condensed milk, egg, cinnamon, ginger, and nutmeg until well blended.

» Roll out the dough on a floured board to about ⅛-inch thickness. Cut into 4-inch circles. In the center of each circle, place about 2 tablespoons of filling and top with a piece of chocolate. Fold the crust over, forming a semicircle, and seal the edges using a little water and a fork to crimp. Place on an ungreased baking sheet and brush the top of each empanada with a little beaten egg, then sprinkle with a little sugar.

» Bake for 45 minutes or until golden brown. Serve warm.

Makes about 16

Caramel Apple Empanadas

FOR SWEET EMPANADAS, you can make them with any kind of fruit. This is one favorite filling, especially in the fall during apple season. Use slightly tart pie apples, such as Granny Smiths or Jonathans. The dulce de leche adds a taste of caramel. You can make it yourself (see below) or buy it premade.

» Make the dough as directed on page 140.

» Peel, core, and dice the apples. In a skillet over medium heat, melt the butter. Add the apples, cinnamon, and brown sugar. Cook, stirring often, until the apples are tender, about 10 minutes.

» Mix the cornstarch with a little cold water to make a paste and add to the apples along with a pinch of salt. Cook until thickened. Remove from heat and cool. Refrigerate for one hour so that the filling thickens.

» Fill the empanadas with the apple mixture and a drizzle of dulce de leche, and then bake as directed on page 140, sprinkling with a little dash of cinnamon in addition to the sugar.

» To serve, place two warm empanadas on a serving plate and drizzle with dulce de leche.

5 medium apples

2 tablespoons butter

1½ teaspoons cinnamon

½ cup brown sugar

2 tablespoons cornstarch

Pinch of salt

½ cup dulce de leche

DULCE DE LECHE

Dulce de leche is basically sweetened milk cooked until it's thick and caramelized. Like its cousin *cajeta*, which is made with goat milk, dulce de leche is a sweet treat used for topping toast, bread, ice cream, fruit, and even dessert tamales.

The easiest way to make it is to start with a can of sweetened condensed milk. Check the label. This isn't the same as evaporated milk, and if you get them mixed up, you won't end up with anything that's fit to eat. Remove the label from the can and set it in a pan of water deep enough to cover the can by two inches. Bring to a boil and simmer for 2-3 hours. Make sure the can stays covered by water at all times. The longer it cooks, the darker the sauce. Remove the pan from the heat and drain the water. Allow the can to cool, then open with a can opener. Store for up to a week in a glass jar in the refrigerator.

Sopaipillas

4 cups unbleached flour

2 teaspoons baking powder

1 teaspoon salt

4 tablespoons shortening or lard

1 egg, beaten

1 to 1½ cups cold water

Oil for frying

SOMETIMES SPELLED "SOPAPILLAS," these golden puffs are a true delicacy from New Mexico. They can be served as a bread or a dessert—as soon as possible after they come out of the frying pan.

» Combine the flour, baking powder, and salt. Blend in the shortening using two knives, a pastry blender, or your fingers. Add the egg and mix in enough water to make a smooth dough. Cover and let it rest for 15 minutes. Then roll it between your palms into 6 equal balls and keep them covered.

» Heat 1-2 inches of oil in a large skillet, usually at about medium high. On a floured board, roll the dough balls into 6-inch rounds, ⅛-inch thick.

Cut them in half with a sharp knife and pierce them slightly in the center with a fork tine or knife point. Then place them very carefully in the hot oil. Baste them with a little hot oil to help them swell, then watch carefully and turn once as the sopaipillas puff up and turn a golden brown. Drain them on paper towels and serve hot with butter and honey.

Yields about a dozen

Natillas

4 egg yolks

2 tablespoons cornstarch

Salt

1 cup sugar, divided

2½ cups fresh milk

1 teaspoon vanilla

4 egg whites (see note on raw eggs page 147)

½ teaspoon cream of tartar

Freshly grated nutmeg

Ground cinnamon

NATILLAS *IS THE NAME FOR A DELICATE EGG CUSTARD* with a meringue *gently folded into it, then topped with a light dusting of freshly grated nutmeg and cinnamon. It is an old-fashioned specialty of northern New Mexico.*

» Thoroughly combine the egg yolks, cornstarch, a dash of salt, and ½ cup of sugar in a medium saucepan. Add the milk and cook over medium heat, stirring constantly, until the mixture has thickened to the consistency of custard. Remove the pan from the heat, add vanilla, and set aside.

» Beat the egg whites and cream of tartar into soft peaks and gradually add the remaining ½ cup of sugar to make a meringue.

» When the custard mixture has cooled, gently fold in the meringue, saving some meringue for decoration if you like. Serve in a bowl or individual cups, sprinkling the nutmeg and cinnamon on top. Natillas can be served immediately or chilled briefly, but it does not keep for very long.

Serves 6–8

Fresh Fruit Ice

WHEN THE TEMPERATURE IN THE DESERT SOARS to what feels like an intolerable level, there's nothing better for cooling down than a scoop of fruit ice made with fresh fruit. The process is easy. Start with simple syrup, add the fruit juice or puree of your choice, and freeze for several hours. Fruit ices are a healthy alternative to ice cream, and if you want to dress them up for the adults in the party, you can include a splash of tequila or liqueur. We've included a few variations below, but use your imagination. How about cantaloupe mint? Or blueberry peach? Just remember that when you choose a tart fruit, use a little more sugar in the syrup.

Simple syrup: Combine the sugar and water in a heavy saucepan over medium heat. Stir until the sugar has completely dissolved. Remove from the heat and set aside to cool.

» Puree the fruit in a blender until smooth. Combine the simple syrup, fruit puree, and/or juices and zest, and pour into a 9 x 13 x 2-inch pan. Cover and place in the freezer.

» After an hour, use a fork to stir the mixture, breaking up any frozen chunks. Return to the freezer and after another hour, repeat the process. Return the pan to the freezer and allow to freeze for at least another six hours.

» To serve, remove the pan from the freezer and allow to sit at room temperature for 5 minutes. Using a fork, scrape the ice from the pan and place in serving bowls. Garnish with fresh mint, a strip of lemon or lime peel, or a fresh strawberry.

» To store, place in an airtight container and freeze for up to six weeks.

Serves 6

Lemon Lime

¾ cup sugar

2¼ cups water

¼ cup fresh lime juice

¼ cup fresh lemon juice

Finely grated zest (page 132) of 2 limes and 1 lemon

Watermelon Strawberry

½ cup sugar

2 cups water

2 cups chopped seedless watermelon

1 pint fresh strawberries, sliced (tops removed)

Juice of 1 lime

Pineapple

½ cup sugar

2 cups water

1 pineapple, peeled, cored, and chopped

Helado Azteca

(Chocolate-Chile Ice Cream)

2 cups heavy cream

1 cup whole milk

6 egg yolks

⅓ cup dark brown sugar, firmly packed

1 teaspoon pure red chile powder

2 ounces unsweetened chocolate, chopped

6 ounces premium bittersweet chocolate, chopped

2 teaspoons ground cinnamon

2 tablespoons coffee liqueur (page 162)

FIRST, YOU EXPERIENCE THE SENSATION of cold, and then the rich taste of chocolate floods your mouth. Finally, you get a nice warm tingle. It's a wonderful experience in contrasts.

» In a heavy saucepan, combine the cream and milk. Bring to a simmer.

» Beat together the egg yolks, brown sugar, and chile powder until fluffy. Pour about ½ cup of the hot milk into the egg yolk mixture, whisking constantly. Add the egg yolk mixture to the hot milk and cook over low heat, stirring constantly until the temperature reaches 170 degrees F on a candy thermometer. Remove from heat.

» Melt the unsweetened and bittersweet chocolates. Strain the custard mixture into the melted chocolate and stir until combined. Stir in the cinnamon and coffee liqueur. Allow to cool, and then freeze according to your ice cream maker instructions.

Makes 1 ½ quarts

Arroz con Leche y Chocolate (Chocolate Rice Pudding)

TRY THE CLASSIC PUDDING in this dark, rich, Southwestern version.

When using eggs raw, it is important to take care to prevent salmonella contamination. Make sure the eggs are fresh and from a safe source and the shells are clean and undamaged. To separate, rather than rocking the yolk back and forth between the shell halves, use one hand to crack the egg into your other hand over a bowl. Allow the whites to run between your fingers into the bowl, and then put the yolk into a separate bowl. You can also crack the egg onto a plate and use a plastic water bottle to suck up the yolk. This reduces the chance of the shell coming into contact with the egg. Another option would be pasteurized eggs, if you can find them.

» In a saucepan over high heat, bring the rice, cinnamon stick, and water to a boil. Reduce heat, cover, and cook until the rice is dry, about 30 minutes. Remove the cinnamon stick.

» Beat together the sugar, melted chocolate, egg yolks, and milk until combined. Add to the rice and cook over medium heat, stirring constantly, until the mixture is thickened. Remove from heat. Beat the egg whites until stiff, and then gently fold into the rice mixture. Serve warm.

Serves 4

1 cup uncooked medium or short grain rice

1 cinnamon stick

2 cups water

½ cup sugar

4 ounces premium bittersweet chocolate, melted and slightly cooled

3 eggs, separated

1 cup milk

Adobe Mud Pie

30 chocolate sandwich cookies
  (such as Oreos), crushed

½ cup butter, melted

½ gallon coffee ice cream

4 ounces unsweetened chocolate

2 tablespoons butter

1 cup sugar

1 can evaporated milk

1 teaspoon vanilla extract

2 cups heavy cream

¼ cup confectioners' sugar

¼ cup coffee liqueur (page 162)

¾ cup semisweet chocolate chips

EL CORRAL IS A TUCSON INSTITUTION, known for prime rib and adobe mud pie. This superb combination of ice cream, coffee, and chocolate is a re-creation of their masterpiece.

» Butter a 9 x 13-inch baking pan. Combine the crushed cookies and melted butter; then press into the bottom of the pan. Chill until firm.

» Soften the ice cream to a spreadable consistency. Spread evenly over the cookie crust and freeze until solid.

» In a heat-proof bowl placed over a pot of simmering water, melt the chocolate and 2 tablespoons butter.

» Add the sugar and milk to a medium heavy saucepan and bring to a boil, stirring constantly. Add the melted chocolate mixture and continue to stir until thickened. Remove from heat and add the vanilla. Cool to room temperature.

» Remove the ice cream pan from the freezer and spread the cooled chocolate sauce over the top. Freeze again until solid.

» Chill a mixing bowl and beaters. Add the cold cream to the bowl and beat at high speed until soft peaks form. Add the sugar and coffee liqueur, and then beat until the peaks are stiff. Spread over the chocolate layer and sprinkle with chocolate chips. Freeze again until firm.

» To serve, remove from the freezer and allow to soften slightly, about 10 minutes. Dip a knife in hot water and cut into pieces. Use a warm spatula to remove the pieces from the pan.

Serves 24

Flan

THIS IS A GREAT PARTY DESSERT, especially after a spicy meal.

1¼ cup sugar, divided

⅓ cup water

2½ cups whole milk

3 eggs

3 egg yolks

1 teaspoon vanilla extract

Caramel: If your large flan mold is stovetop-safe, you can cook the caramel directly in it. If not, use a small saucepan. (To help the caramel spread evenly, warm porcelain or glass molds while you caramelize the sugar.)

» Swirl ¾ cup sugar and water over medium-high heat until the sugar dissolves. Boil the syrup, swirling occasionally, for 3–5 minutes, or until it starts to change color. Watch carefully; it will turn from clear to yellow to gold to light brown. You want a rich amber brown, but remember that the caramel will continue to darken briefly off the heat.

» When you think the color is brown enough, either tilt the mold to cover the inside with caramel, or pour it into the warmed molds and quickly tilt to coat. Set aside while you prepare the flan.

» Preheat the oven to 325 degrees F.

Flan: In a small saucepan, warm the milk just until it starts to steam. Also bring a kettle of water to a simmer to use as a water bath to bake the flan.

» Beat the eggs and yolks together in a medium mixing bowl, gradually add the remaining ½ cup sugar, and whisk until the mixture is light. Still beating, slowly add the hot milk and vanilla. Set the prepared mold in a roasting pan and strain in the mixture. Pull out the oven rack, set the pan on it, and pour enough simmering water into the pan to reach halfway up the sides of the mold.

» Bake until the flan is barely set and a skewer inserted in the center comes out clean. Watch carefully. If you see any bubbles in the water bath, add cool water. Baking time varies from 20–30 minutes for small custard cups to over an hour for large, deep flans.

» Cool the flan in its mold on a wire rack, then refrigerate. Flan unmolds best when it has been well chilled. To serve, run the tip of a knife around the edge, place a serving dish (deep enough to catch the caramel sauce) upside down over the mold, and quickly flip the two. The flan should drop neatly onto the dish. If it does not, dip the mold in warm water for a moment or two, and try again. Scrape out remaining caramel, spoon it around the flan, and serve.

Makes a 1-quart flan or 6 individual 6-ounce flans

Orange Flan

THIS WILL FEED A CROWD, so make it a day or two in advance of your special occasion. Hold it in the baking dish in the refrigerator, and then unmold it and add the mandarin oranges and fresh raspberries just before serving.

» Preheat the oven to 325 degrees F.

» Pour the sugar into a heavy, medium skillet. Place the skillet over medium heat until the sugar begins to melt. Reduce the heat to low and, without stirring, allow the sugar to melt and turn golden-brown. Working quickly, pour the resulting caramel over the bottom of a 3-quart glass baking dish, tilting to spread up the sides.

» In a large bowl, whisk the eggs until blended and then whisk in the sweetened condensed milk, whole milk, vanilla, orange extract, salt, and liqueur. Blend until smooth. Strain the mixture into the prepared baking dish. Cover the dish with foil. Place a large roasting pan of warm water on the oven's middle rack. Set the baking dish into the roasting pan. The water should reach half the depth of the baking dish.

» Bake for 1½ hours until the center feels just firm when pressed. Remove from the water bath and cool on a wire rack to room temperature, then refrigerate until serving.

» To serve, run a knife around the edges of the baking dish. Place a large serving platter over the dish and turn both upside down. Gently shake the dish to release the flan. Use the drained mandarin slices to create flowers on the top of the flan, using the raspberries for the centers.

Serves 12–15

1½ cups sugar

8 eggs

2 cans (14 ounces each) sweetened condensed milk (not evaporated)

1¼ cups whole milk

1 teaspoon vanilla

1 teaspoon orange extract

¼ teaspoon salt

2 tablespoons Grand Marnier or other orange liqueur (page 163)

2 cans mandarin oranges, drained, for garnish

Raspberries, for garnish

Tres Leches Cake

Cake

1½ cups all-purpose flour

2 teaspoons baking powder

½ teaspoon salt

6 eggs, separated

½ teaspoon cream of tartar

1 cup sugar

⅓ cup cold water

2 teaspoons vanilla extract

1 teaspoon almond extract

Three Milks

1 can (14 ounces) condensed milk

1 small can (5 ounces) evaporated milk

1 cup heavy cream

2 teaspoons vanilla extract, or 1 tablespoon rum or brandy

Ingredient list continued on following page

"THREE MILKS" CAKE IS A RECENT ARRIVAL in the United States—whether from Nicaragua, Guatemala, or Mexico is unclear. The tres leches that go into this lavish treat are condensed milk, evaporated milk, and heavy cream. The cake is sweet and rich—and extremely white—so tart, colorful fruits greatly enhance it. Covered and refrigerated, Tres Leches Cake keeps well for a day or two, either before or after the frosting goes on, so it's also a good dessert to make ahead for a special occasion.

» Line a greased 9 x 13-inch baking pan with parchment or wax paper. Grease and flour the pan, including the paper. Preheat the oven to 350 degrees F.

» Whisk together the flour, baking powder, and salt in a medium mixing bowl. In a larger bowl, beat the 6 egg whites until they are foamy. Add the cream of tartar and continue to whip until soft peaks form.

» In another large bowl, beat the egg yolks until they are light and thick. Still beating, gradually add the sugar, and continue whipping until the mixture forms a slowly dissolving ribbon when dripped from the beater. Then add the cold water and vanilla and almond extracts to the yolk mixture, followed by the flour mixture. Delicately fold the beaten egg whites into the batter.

» Scrape the batter into the prepared pan and smooth the top. Bake the cake for 25-30 minutes, or until its center is lightly springy and a cake tester or toothpick comes out clean. Allow the cake to cool to room temperature in the pan (about 20 minutes).

» Then run a knife around the sides of the pan, cover with a deep serving platter with a lip to contain the three milks, and carefully invert the cake onto the platter. Prick the surface of the cake all over with a fork.

» Three Milks: While the cake cools, mix the condensed milk, evaporated milk, cream, and vanilla (or rum or brandy) in a 1-quart measuring pitcher. After the cake is removed from the pan, pour the liquid over it bit by bit, cover it, and refrigerate for several hours or overnight. When the cake has absorbed the three milks, it is ready to frost and serve.

» Meringue Frosting: In a large mixing bowl or stationary mixer, beat the egg whites with the salt until foamy. Then add the cream of tartar and beat until soft peaks form.

Meringue Frosting

4 egg whites

⅛ teaspoon salt

¼ teaspoon cream of tartar

½ cup water

¾ cup sugar

3 tablespoons light corn syrup

1 teaspoon vanilla extract

Fresh fruit for serving, such as strawberries, raspberries, blueberries, peaches, pineapple, mangoes, or a mixture

» Bring the water, sugar, and corn syrup to a boil in a small saucepan. Cover the pan and boil over medium heat for 2–3 minutes to wash down any sugar crystals from the sides of the pan. Then uncover the pan and continue to boil until the temperature of the sugar syrup reaches 240 degrees F on a candy thermometer, or the soft-ball stage (a few drops will form a malleable shape in a cup of cold water).

» Immediately move the syrup from the heat, begin to beat the egg whites on low speed, and dribble the syrup slowly over them, avoiding the beater itself, which will spatter. When all the syrup has been added, raise the speed to high and beat the meringue for 2–3 minutes, or until it's cool and glossy. Blend in the vanilla. Frost the top and sides of the cake, and garnish with fruit just before serving.

Serves 15

Mexican Chocolate Torte

Crust

1½ cups graham cracker crumbs

½ cup cocoa

½ cup sugar

5 tablespoons butter, melted

½ teaspoon ground cinnamon

½ teaspoon hot New Mexico chile powder

1 teaspoon salt

Cooking spray

Filling

12 ounces semi-sweet chocolate chips

3 eggs

¼ cup sugar

1 teaspoon vanilla

½ teaspoon ground cinnamon

½ teaspoon hot New Mexico chile powder

½ teaspoon salt

1 cup heavy cream

USE A PREMIUM CHOCOLATE IN COMBINATION with "real" cinnamon (Cinnamomum verum, or canela in Spanish, not the cassia sold in most grocery spice sections) for a taste experience that would have made Montezuma sigh in satisfaction.

» For the crust, blend together the graham cracker crumbs, cocoa, sugar, butter, cinnamon, chile powder, and salt. Press firmly into the bottom of a 9-inch springform pan that has been sprayed lightly with cooking spray.

» For the filling, place the chocolate chips, eggs, sugar, vanilla, cinnamon, chile powder, and salt in a blender. Heat the cream to a rapid simmer and then pour it into the chocolate mixture with the blender running. Blend until smooth.

» Pour the filling into the crust. Refrigerate or freeze for at least 4 hours. Can be frozen for up to 1 month.

» Allow to sit at room temperature for 30 minutes before serving. Serve with whipped cream and fresh berries.

Makes a 9-inch cake (serves 12–16)

Traditional Mexican Hot Chocolate

THE HAPPIER THE COOK, the frothier the chocolate. At least that's what they say. If you want to be a real traditionalist, use a wooden molinillo *to add the froth. And if you want to spice things up a little, add a pinch of chile powder to the pan.*

» In a heavy saucepan, heat the milk. Add the grated chocolate, stirring occasionally until melted. Remove from heat, add the vanilla, and then, using an immersion blender or wire whisk, whip the hot chocolate until frothy. Pour into mugs and add cinnamon stick stirrers.

Serves 4

4 cups whole milk

1 tablet (3 ounces) Mexican chocolate, grated

2 teaspoons vanilla extract

4 cinnamon sticks

DRINKS

LIQUEURS, COCKTAILS, WINE, AND BEER are all fitting accompaniments to most Southwest dishes. Alcohol will cut down on the feel of spicy chiles in your mouth, and the crisp, refreshing flavors of the drinks complement the richness of the food. And then there's the festive aspect of gathering a group of friends or neighbors together for margaritas and guacamole on the patio on a warm summer evening.

Liqueurs in the Southwest are usually based on citrus fruits or coffee. Kahlúa is probably the best known of the coffee liqueurs made in Mexico, and it's very easy to make your own version at home. It just takes a little patience, since most liqueurs require a month or more of aging before they're ready to drink. Triple sec is an orange liqueur typically used in margaritas—it's a blend of orange peel and clear alcohol, which is also easy to make yourself. Grand Marnier, also commonly used in margaritas, is an orange brandy-based liqueur with a slightly more complex flavor than triple sec.

The Southwest is home to a burgeoning wine industry, with regions in Arizona, New Mexico, southern California, and Colorado—and Sonora and Baja California as well. It's always a fun weekend adventure to drive through the various wine-producing areas, sampling the offerings of the local vintners, but if you want to do something festive at home, make sangria. It's a drink with origins in Spain, but it's been adopted throughout the Southwest as a favorite summertime party drink.

And then there's beer. Lots of local craft breweries are popping up all over the Southwest, but Mexican beers are still a favorite, served ice cold with a dash of salt and a squeeze of lime. Or you can try beer cocktails like the michelada.

There's no pretension with spirits in Southwest cuisine. Drink what tastes good and don't be afraid to get creative.

Michelada

1 cup tomato juice

½ teaspoon Tabasco sauce

½ teaspoon Worcestershire sauce

Juice of two limes

½ teaspoon chile powder

Ice

2 bottles Mexican beer such as Corona or Pacifico

IF YOU DON'T WANT THE HEAVY ALCOHOL OF A BLOODY MARY but would also like to spice up your beer, this is your answer. This drink comes from Morelia, Mexico, but it has become increasingly popular along the border. Adjust the seasonings as you desire to make it very hot, or not.

» Prepare two tumblers with salt/chile rims (page 159).

» In cocktail shaker, mix together tomato juice, Tabasco sauce, Worcestershire sauce, lime juice, chile powder, and ice. Divide evenly between the prepared glasses, then fill the glasses with beer. Garnish with a slice of lime.

Serves 2

VARIATION *Cerveza con Limonada*

» If you'd like to keep things even simpler, fill a glass with ice, then add enough limeade (page 125) or lemonade to fill it halfway. Fill the rest with beer and garnish with lime.

The Perfect Margarita

JIMMY BUFFETT MAY CRAVE "THAT FROZEN CONCOCTION," but this is a much more refined version than what you'll find in a Parrothead bar. Use the best tequila you can afford, serve on the rocks, and sip away to paradise.

» Rub the lime wedge around the rim of the glass and then dip the rim in the salt. Add cracked ice to the glass.

» Combine the tequila, Grand Marnier, and lime and orange juices in a cocktail shaker with a few ice cubes. Shake well; then pour into the salted glass filled with cracked ice. Squeeze the lime wedge into the glass.

Serves 1

1 lime wedge

1 tablespoon kosher salt

Cracked ice

1 ounce premium tequila plata (silver or white, sometimes called blanco)

1 ounce Grand Marnier

2 ounces fresh lime juice

2 ounces fresh orange juice

Ice cubes

BASIC COCKTAIL RIM

One thing that makes a simple cocktail special is the sparkle and extra boost of flavor that comes from a creative rim garnish. Add a little spice to your next Bloody Mary, martini, or even a classic fresh-squeezed lemonade. Mix two parts kosher salt with one part chile powder. If you're making a sweet drink, use sugar instead of salt. Play with different salts and sugars for different textures and flavors. It's important to moisten the rim of the glass before dipping into the dry mixture. The most common method is to run a wedge of lemon or lime around the rim before dipping. You could also use simple syrup or, for an even sexier look, try honey. (The honey runs down the glass and looks very cool, although it is just a touch messy.) Any leftover salt or sugar mixture can be stored in a tightly covered container for up to a month.

Sangria Blanca

2 lemons

2 limes

2 oranges

2 cups water

1 cup sugar

1 bottle (1½ liters) dry white wine

¼ cup triple sec or other orange liqueur

1 quart club soda

Crushed ice

USE A CRISP, YET INEXPENSIVE, Sauvignon Blanc to blend with the citrus flavors. This is a festive party drink, especially when you serve it in a glass pitcher where the colors of the fruit shine through.

» Slice the lemons, limes, and oranges, reserving the ends. Wrap the slices in plastic wrap and refrigerate.

» Place the ends in a saucepan with the water and sugar. Bring to a boil over medium heat and cook until the sugar dissolves, about 5 minutes. Remove from heat and cool. Remove the fruit pieces and then strain.

» In a large pitcher or punch bowl, combine the sugar syrup, triple sec, and wine. Add sliced oranges and lemons, then pour in the club soda. Serve over crushed ice.

Serves 8

VARIATION Sangria Roja

AS PRETTY AS IT IS TASTY, this makes a great summer party drink. The recipe easily doubles for a crowd.

» Follow the recipe for Sangria Blanca, but use 5 lemons and 3 oranges in place of the citrus, and add ½ cup brandy to a 1½-liter bottle of dry red wine.

Mocha Buzz

Mocha Buzz

¾ cup milk

¾ cup half-and-half

4 ounces premium bittersweet
   chocolate, finely chopped

2 shots espresso

2 shots coffee liqueur (page 162)

A GREAT DRINK FOR BRUNCH on a cold winter morning.

» In a saucepan, heat the milk and half-and-half just to a simmer. Add the chocolate and stir to melt. Remove from heat and stir in the espresso and liqueur. Pour into mugs.

Serves 2

Spicy Maria

Spicy Maria

1 quart tomato juice

½ cup fresh lemon juice

2 tablespoons horseradish

1 teaspoon Rose's lime juice

1 teaspoon Worcestershire sauce

½ teaspoon hot pepper sauce

1½ cups vodka

Cracked ice

Freshly ground black pepper

6 lime wedges

12 jalapeño-stuffed green olives

6 celery ribs, leafy tops intact

SPECIALTY FOOD STORES USUALLY CARRY A WIDE VARIETY of hot sauces with differing levels of heat. Experiment until you find one that suits your taste. If you like it really spicy, use extra-hot horseradish.

» Combine the tomato juice, lemon juice, horseradish, lime juice, Worcestershire sauce, and hot pepper sauce in a large pitcher, stirring well. Add the vodka and stir again. Pour into glasses filled with ice. Sprinkle each drink with black pepper to taste, then garnish with 1 lime wedge and 2 olives on a toothpick, along with one celery rib.

Serves 6

Mexican Coffee

BUY THE SMALLEST BOTTLES OF SEVERAL BRANDS of coffee liqueur to find the one you like best; many prefer Kahlúa, which is made with Mexican coffee beans. You can also make your own, using the recipe below.

» Pour the coffee liqueur into a serving mug. Fill with hot, brewed coffee and sugar to taste. Garnish with whipped cream, if desired.

Serves 1

Mexican Coffee

1½ ounces Mexican coffee liqueur

1 cup hot, brewed coffee

Sugar

Whipped cream for garnish (optional)

Coffee Liqueur

IT TAKES A WHILE FOR THE FLAVORS TO DEVELOP, but it's worth the wait. This liqueur makes an ideal do-ahead holiday gift. Decorative, food-safe bottles can be purchased at gourmet shops or the housewares section of department and specialty stores. You'll need bottles with lids such as screw-on caps or tight-fitting corks to help prevent evaporation.

» Clean and sterilize two 26-ounce glass bottles. Set aside.

» In a large, heatproof bowl, mix the espresso powder and sugar. Stir in the boiling water until the sugar is dissolved. Allow to cool to room temperature. Add the vodka.

» Split the vanilla bean in half and add one half to each of the prepared bottles. Divide the coffee liqueur evenly between the 2 bottles. Close the bottles tightly. Keep in a cool, dark place for at least a month before serving.

Makes about 6 ½ cups

Coffee Liqueur

2 ounces espresso powder

3½ cups sugar

2 cups boiling water

1 pint vodka

1 whole vanilla bean

Orange Liqueur

4 pounds Valencia or blood oranges

1 750-ml bottle of vodka or grain alcohol

6 cups water

6 cups sugar

THIS IS SIMILAR TO TRIPLE SEC, and can be used to make margaritas or sipped like a cordial. Keep it in the freezer so that it's always icy cold and ready to drink. This is another one that requires a little patience, so don't be tempted to open it too soon. Give the orange peel time to turn loose its flavor.

» Wash the oranges well and remove just the peel, taking care to avoid removing the pith from the oranges along with the peel. The pith will make the liqueur bitter. Juice the oranges for another use. Place the peel in a large glass jar with a tight-fitting lid and pour in the vodka. Cover and keep in a dark, cool place for one month.

» At the end of the month, strain the peels out of the vodka and discard the peels. In a large pot over medium heat, mix the water and sugar and bring to a simmer to make a simple syrup. Cook for about ten minutes until the sugar is completely dissolved. Remove from heat and cool.

» Add the simple syrup to the orange-infused vodka and stir. Return to a large glass jar, cover tightly, and let sit for another week. You can leave it in the jar or pour into sterilized decorative bottles with stoppers to give as gifts.

Makes 2 quarts

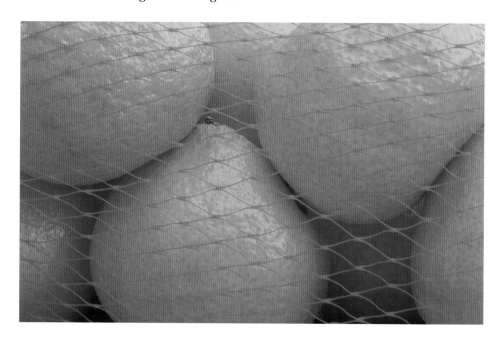

SOURCES FOR SOUTHWESTERN INGREDIENTS

Cheri's Desert Harvest

Retail and online sales of prickly pear, agave, mesquite, citrus, and pomegranate syrup, as well as jellies, candies, honey, and mixes.

1840 E Winsett St
Tucson, AZ 85719
(520) 623-4141
www.cherisdesertharvest.com

The Chile Guy

Online retail and wholesale chile products, spices, and herbs.

168 E Calle Don Francisco
Bernalillo, NM 87004
(800) 869-9218
www.thechileguy.com

Fiesta Stores

Retail grocery chain in Houston, Dallas, and Austin.

2300 N Shepherd Dr
Houston, TX 77063
(713) 869-6188
www.fiestamart.com

The Great American Spice Co.

Very large assortment of spices available online.

2300 Meyer Rd
Fort Wayne, IN 46803
(877) 677-4239
www.americanspice.com

Hatch Chile Express

New Mexico farm family sells frozen and dried Hatch chile products, green and red.

P.O. Box 350
Hatch, NM 87937
(800) 292-4454
www.hatch-chile.com

Kalustyan's

Huge selection of spices from around the world. Both retail and online sales.

123 Lexington Ave
New York, NY 10016
(212) 685-3451
www.kalustyans.com

La Michoacana Meat Market

Largest Hispanic grocery chain in the United States with more than 100 locations throughout Texas.

1413 Gessner Dr
Houston, TX 77043
(713) 461-7302
www.lamichoacanameatmarket.com

LatinMerchant.com

Online store for El Mercado Latino, located in Seattle's Pike Place Market. Foods, seasonings, condiments, and cooking equipment from all across Latin America and the American Southwest.

1514 Pike Pl
Suite 6
Seattle, WA 98101
(206) 223-9374
www.latinmerchant.com

Lowe's

Retail grocery chain in Texas, New Mexico, and Colorado.

www.supersfoods.com

SOURCES FOR SOUTHWESTERN INGREDIENTS

Mexgrocer.com

National online grocery for Mexican food products, cooking equipment, and health and beauty products.

4060 Morena Blvd
Suite C
San Diego, CA 92117
(877) 463-9476
www.mexgrocer.com

Mi Pueblo Food Center

Mexican grocery chain with locations throughout Northern California.

1775 Story Rd
San Jose, CA 95122
(888) 997-7717
www.mipueblo.com

Native Seeds/SEARCH

Nonprofit organization sells heirloom seeds, beans, dried chiles, chile and mole powders, corn products, grains, teas, sauces, and sweets.

3061 N Campbell Ave
Tucson, AZ 85719
(866) 622-5561
www.nativeseeds.org

Penzey's Spices

Wide array of spices available in retail stores as well as online and by mail order.

12001 W Capitol Dr
Wauwatosa, WI 53222
(800) 741-7787
www.penzeys.com

Rancho Gordo New World Specialty Food

Heirloom beans, dried corn products, chile products, grains, rice, herbs, and spices.

1924 Yajome St
Napa, CA 94559
(707) 259-1935
www.ranchogordo.com

Santa Cruz Chili & Spice Co.

Retail shop, commercial products, and online retail sales of chile paste, powder, sauces, seasonings, spices, and herbs.

1868 E Frontage Rd
Tumacacori-Carmen, AZ 85640
(520) 398-2591
www.santacruzchili.com

Santa Fe School of Cooking

Retail shop and online sales of chiles, cooking tools, foods, herbs, and spices.

125 N Guadalupe St
Santa Fe, NM 87501
(505) 983-4511
www.santafeschoolofcooking.com

Savory Spice Shop

Retail stores in several states and on-line spices, herbs, chile powders, salts, flavorings, and other specialty items.

1537 Platte St
Denver, CO 80202
(303) 477-3322
www.savoryspiceshop.com

RECIPE SOURCES

Most of the recipes in this collection were adapted from the following cookbooks—all published by Rio Nuevo Publishers—and the remaining recipes were contributed by the editors. Many thanks to all of our authors for their generosity and kitchen wisdom.

From *Flora's Kitchen*
by Regina Romero (1998)
» Biscochitos
» Chicken Tostadas
» Chiles Rellenos
» Flour Tortillas
» Fry Bread
» Nachos
» Natillas
» Navajo Tacos with Fry Bread
» Sopaipillas
» Spanish Rice
» Taquitos with Chicken (or Beef)

From *Clouds for Dessert*
by Susan Lowell (2004)
» Flan
» Tres Leches Cake

From *Absolutely Avocado*
by Geraldine Duncann (2006)
» Chile and Cheese Avocado Soup
» Quick and Easy Chicken Avocado Fajitas

From *Chile Aphrodisia*
by Amy Reilly and Annette Tomei (2006)
» Chile Corn Chowder
» Chile-Spiced Grilled Fruit
» Green Chile Eggs Benny
» Jalapeño Limeade
» Mexican Chocolate Torte

From *Cilantro Secrets*
by Gwyneth Doland (2006)
» Bison Burgers with Pepita Pesto
» Calabacitas
» Flank Steak with Creamy Rajas
» Green Rice
» Grilled Corn with Compound Butter
» Migas
» Pico de Gallo
» Roasted Chicken with Cilantro-Lime Rub
» Spanish Black Beans
» Squash Blossom Quesadillas
» Tomato Soup with Corn Salsa

From *Citrus Essentials*
by Marilyn Noble (2006)
» Carne Asada Tacos with Pico de Gallo
» Ceviche
» Chicken with Tequila Lime Marinade
» Cornhusk Salmon
» Easy Guacamole
» Jalapeño Lime Barbecue Sauce
» Lemon Chicken Topopo
» Mango Peach Salsa
» The Perfect Margarita
» Prickly Pear Lemonade
» Sangria Blanca
» Sangria Roja
» Spicy Maria

From *Gorgeous Garlic*
by Gwin Grogan Grimes (2006)
» Corn Bisque with Garlic and Chiles
» Garlic Cheese-Stuffed Jalapeño Peppers
» Garlic Chile con Queso
» Garlic Roasted Asparagus with Orange Zest
» Grilled Chicken with Garlic-Chipotle Barbecue Sauce
» Grilled Fish with Roasted Tomato and Garlic Sauce
» Jicama Pineapple Salad
» Roasted Garlic Quesadillas
» Shrimp Mojo de Ajo
» Cheese Quesadillas

From *¡Mole!*
by Gwyneth Doland (2006)
» Chicken Wings in Mole
» Grilled Flank or Skirt Steak with Mole Verde
» Huevos Rancheros
» Mole Verde
» Steak Burritos with Nopalitos
» Turkey Mole Burgers

From *Nuts*
by Gwin Grogran Grimes (2006)
» Piñon Cookies

RECICE SOURCES

From *Seductive Salsa*
by Gwyneth Doland (2006)
» Black Bean Salsa
» Fresh Corn Salsa
» Salsa de Molcajete

From *The Healthy Southwest Table* by Janet Taylor (2007)
» Tangy Tuna Cabbage Salad

From *Tantalizing Tamales*
by Gwyneth Doland (2007)
» Basic Masa
» Green Chile Chicken Tamales
» Green Corn Tamales with Green Chile
» Pork and Red Chile Tamales

From *Coffee Creations*
by Gwin Grogan Grimes (2008)
» Cocoa-Coffee Spice Rub
» Coffee Barbecue Sauce
» Coffee Fajita Marinade
» Coffee Liqueur
» Espresso-Chile Steak Rub
» Mexican Coffee

From *Viva Chocolate!*
by Marilyn Noble (2008)
» Adobe Mud Pie
» Arroz con Leche y Chocolate (Chocolate Rice Pudding)
» Chocolate Pumpkin Empanadas
» Helado Azteca (Chocolate-Chile Ice Cream)
» Mocha Buzz
» Pecan Chile Chicken
» Traditional Mexican Hot Chocolate

From *Southwest Comfort Food*
by Marilyn Noble (2011)
» Albóndigas
» Black Bean Soup
» Chicken Enchiladas with Red Chile Sauce
» Cowboy Pinto Beans
» Grilled Orange Turkey
» Lamb Stew
» Orange Flan
» Red Chile Pork Posole
» Refritos (Refried Beans)
» Sopa de Frijoles
» Southwest Corn Bread

From *The Green Southwest Cookbook* by Janet Taylor (2012)
» Agua Fresca de Melón o Sandía
» Agua Fresca de Tamarindo

INDEX